Happiness and Well-Being in Islam

Sálua Omais

Happiness and Well-Being in Islam

Intersections Between Positive Psychology, Psychology of Religion and Islamic Psychology

 Springer

Sálua Omais (iD)
Campo Grande, Mato Grosso do Sul, Brazil

ISBN 978-3-031-95352-1   ISBN 978-3-031-95353-8   (eBook)
https://doi.org/10.1007/978-3-031-95353-8

This Springer imprint is published by the registered company Springer Nature Switzerland AG
The registered company address is: Gewerbestrasse 11, 6330 Cham, Switzerland

If disposing of this product, please recycle the paper.

بِسْمِ اللَّهِ الرَّحْمَٰنِ الرَّحِيمِ

In the Name of God, Most Gracious, Most Merciful

إِنَّ اللَّهَ لَا يُغَيِّرُ مَا بِقَوْمٍ حَتَّىٰ يُغَيِّرُوا مَا بِأَنْفُسِهِمْ

Indeed, Allāh will not change the condition of a people until they change what is in themselves (Quran, 13:11)

Preface

The study of happiness and well-being is fundamental to both psychological science and the field of health in general. High levels of well-being generate numerous benefits like improvements in physical health, emotional relationships, interpersonal relationships, resilience, and cognitive functions, as well as having a positive impact on productivity at work, reducing absenteeism, turnover, and conflicts in the organizational environment. Distortions and unrealistic expectations about happiness—focused on immediate gratification or unattainable standards—ultimately result in frustration and sadness. The search for high levels of excitement and success can have the opposite effect, causing people to plunge into even more negative emotional states after peaks of euphoria, with mood swings, depressive symptoms, and feelings of emptiness and loneliness. For this reason, contrary to what many people think, the optimum level of happiness is not reached at the maximum level, at the peak of euphoria, but at moderate and stable levels.

Positive Psychology (PP) is a movement that is still undergoing a process of growth, expansion, and maturation. Over time and with the evolution of PP, the study of well-being gained broader and deeper dimensions that today encompass different peoples, cultures, and worldviews. The fact that most of the knowledge disseminated around the world has been built from a Western perspective has created gaps in science about non-Western people's cultures and worldviews, especially in the field of psychology. This reality has given rise to new epistemological currents, such as the revival of Islamic psychology, which seeks to recover classic knowledge and include new theoretical perspectives on the human psyche in line with Islamic beliefs and values.

The growing interest in investigating well-being in other cultures has gained momentum in recent decades. Although this work was conceived to complement the scientific repertoire of diverse topics linked to Islamic Psychology by focusing on Muslims' beliefs, values, and lifestyle, the topic of well-being in Islam has also aroused interest among Western researchers, both in positive psychology and in the field of the psychology of religion. This includes Martin Seligman himself, leader of the positive psychology movement, who, during the 7th International Positive Psychology Congress (IPPA) in 2021, highlighted the need to expand studies on happiness and well-being from different religious perspectives, including his own interest in learning more about this topic from the perspective of Islam.

Over the years, the knowledge and experience I have acquired in the field of positive psychology has allowed me to have closer contact with the subject of happiness and well-being. In addition to various courses and specializations, in 2018 I had the opportunity to introduce the subject of happiness at the university where I was teaching and also to publish my book *Manual of Positive Psychology* (*Manual de Psicologia Positiva*, original title in Portuguese). All this allowed me to deepen my knowledge and, at the same time, to resume a preliminary project on human virtues and happiness in the view of the Quran that had lain dormant for a considerable length of time. As a Muslim and the daughter of Lebanese immigrants, I have always seen the Quran as an inexhaustible source of psychological knowledge, and of course, since it is a religious and spiritual book, it is more than expected that the Quran's contents have such an intrinsic and connected relationship with the human psyche.

The contents presented in this work are the fruit of my extensive doctoral research, which began in 2019 in Brazil (although it was conceived a few years prior to that). This research gave rise to articles that were published in Brazil. It was also the first scientific study published in Portuguese on this specific subject. Over the years, I have expanded and complemented this research exploring some prophetic traditions of the *Sunnah* which, although broad and numerous, are indispensable for understanding any topic related to Islam. This work also includes some content from *tafseer*, the exegesis of the Qur'an, and works by renowned scholars in the field, both in Islamic philosophy and contemporary Islamic psychology. The construction of this work has brought even broader and deeper dimensions about well-being in Islam, which I have consolidated through analysis and flowcharts that clearly and didactically condense the content researched, especially in the last chapters.

The aim of this book is to contribute to expanding the scientific repertoire, so that this work's contents may add new knowledge and open up new paths in the field of Islamic psychology, providing information and insights that can serve as a basis for the construction of measurement instruments, interventions, and preventive and therapeutic practices in the clinical field, and also in related areas such as education, health, the social field, and organizational environments.

May God accept our efforts, forgive our faults, and make the path easier so that we may achieve well-being and a pleasant life in this life and in the life to come!

Campo Grande, Brazil   Sálua Omais

Acknowledgments

First and foremost, I would like to thank God, the Omniscient, for allowing me to carry out this project from beginning to end — deepening my wisdom and reflections, and further strengthening my admiration for His greatness and the beauty of Islam's teachings. The Prophet Muhammad (ﷺ) teachings and guidance are also endless sources of knowledge. I also lack words to express the immense gratitude I owe to my family for their patience during the time I was involved in the construction of this work, being absent so frequently. My parents, as well as my sister Samira and my brother Maruan were fundamental and indispensable supports for me to be able to focus so intensely on my research work, enabling moments of deep reflection that generated valuable insights for this project. My special thanks also go to my uncle Ahmad, the tireless person who has shared so much knowledge about Islam throughout my life collaborating significantly during the construction of this book. I would like to thank everyone else who has crossed my path, including relatives, friends, professors, researchers, the sheikhs in Brazil, the Cambridge Muslim College and others who contributed directly or indirectly to this work, adding new knowledge over the years as I have researched happiness and well-being in Islam. I would also like to highlight the important role of PsicoIslam, a group formed by Muslim psychologists in Brazil that provides mental health guidance to the community. My special thanks also for the translation work carried out by William Shelton. May this knowledge be useful to all readers, broadening their understanding of the beliefs and way of life of Muslims, opening up new horizons in science based on the wealth of teachings that Islam can provide, especially in the field of Psychology.

Competing Interests The author has no competing interests to declare that are relevant to the content of this manuscript.

Contents

About the Author

Dr. Sálua Omais holds a PhD in Psychology from the University of São Paulo (USP) and has been a visiting doctoral student at both the University of Cambridge and the Cambridge Muslim College (CMC) in United Kingdom. She holds a Master's degree in Health Psychology and Mental Health, an MBA in Positive Psychology and Human Development, a Postgraduate degree in Islamic Psychology from CMC, a Postgraduate degree in Cognitive Behavioral Therapy, and a Bachelor's degree in Psychology. She also has a Bachelor's degree in Law and Dentistry. From 2022 to 2024 Dr. Omais also served as the President of the Religious Freedom and Assistance Commission at OAB/MS (Brazilian Bar Association—Mato Grosso do Sul Section). In the field of Psychology, Dr. Omais has been practicing as a clinical psychologist since 2008 and has also served as a voluntary lecturer at the Federal University of Mato Grosso do Sul, where she implemented the discipline of Happiness and Emotional Intelligence in the Campus. She has published articles about Islam and Islamic Psychology in national and international journals and authored two books in the field of Psychology in Brazil, one of them called *Manual of Positive Psychology*. She has presented her doctoral research at diverse Brazilian and International Conferences including the 6th World Congress on Positive Psychology (IPPA) in Australia, the International Conference on Contemporary Islamic Studies in Malasia, the Annual International Conference of Doctoral Students in Spain, and the Canadian Muslim Mental Health Conference. She has been a member of the International Positive Psychology Association (IPPA) and actually is a member of various institutions such as the National Association of Islamic Jurists (ANAJI), the International Students of Islamic Psychology (ISIP), the International Association for Psychology of Religion (IAPR), and the Al-Balkhi Institute of Islamic Psychological Studies and Research. Dr. Omais performs other professional roles working as a speaker and instructor/facilitator of various courses for both public and private institutions. She also leads a group of Muslim psychologists in Brazil, called PsicoIslam, that provides mental health guidance to the

Muslim community through webinars and educational content on this subject in social media platforms. More contents about her and her work on Positive Psychology can be found in her website *www.psicotrainer.com.br* or *www.saluao-mais.com.br*.

Social Media
Instagram @saluapsicologiapositiva and @psicoislam
Facebook @psicotrainer

List of Figures

Chapter 1
Happiness, Well-Being, and the Positive Psychology Movement

Happiness is a concept that we can define in different ways, depending on the subjective meaning each individual gives it. The word's etymological origin comes from the term "hap," which means chance or fortune, with "happy" being a term denoting good fortune and prosperity, and "ness" a mental state of pleasure and contentment (*Online Etymology Dictionary*, 2024). Although it traverses several fields of knowledge, the philosophy of science was the pioneer in exploring and developing this theme. Thus, we must take a brief look at how ancient thinkers in the Western world explored the subject.

Inquiries and reflections by different thinkers brought together distinct conceptions of happiness' diverse meanings. The rich legacy left by Greek philosophy reached the West thanks to efforts by Muslim philosophers, who translated classical thinkers' seminal works and also developed their own theories during the Middle Ages. Among the highlights of philosophical inquiries into happiness are the Aristotelian concepts of hedonism, represented by sensible pleasure and immediate gratification, and eudaimonism, a concept that understands happiness as the purpose of human actions, obtained through virtue and ethics. However, these virtues should be developed and strengthened through training and practicing in situations that challenge them. Temperance, for example, characterized by abstaining from pleasures, would be strengthened through abstaining from these pleasures and not through immediate satisfaction (Aristotle, 2003).

Aristotelian thought declared that happiness is a purpose in and of itself and the ultimate goal of human actions, being the fruit of the soul's activity aligned with virtue and good deeds. For this reason, there were three different perspectives on happiness: a pleasant life, symbolized by pleasures; a political life, focused on the collective good; and a contemplative life, sustained by wisdom and knowledge. He considers happiness to be conditioned by the practice of virtues in line with what he calls "the highest virtue" (Aristotle, p. 228, 2003). He stated that the sources of happiness would not be hobbies, but a virtuous life achieved through effort and not just pleasure and fun. In order to be happy, it would be necessary to engage in virtuous behavior even if the individual is beset by adversity, bearing life's contingencies with dignity and seeking to make the best of the situation. Such conduct would make the soul nobler and happiness independent of the misfortunes and woes suffered, even in the face of the worst circumstances.

In Aristotelian thought, the dialectic between pain and pleasure would be the basis for moral excellence. Aristotle also warned about the effects of hedonic adaptation, characterized by pleasure's impermanence and fleeting nature. Its intensity is reduced as soon as the desired object ceases to be a novelty. For this reason, pleasure cannot be an end in itself, as it is diluted over time. He explains that the attraction of pleasure would impair our capacity to judge, making intemperance stronger than moderation, since it is from pleasure and the attempt to escape suffering that the subject ends up doing wrong deeds. The fight against pleasure would therefore be more difficult than that against suffering. According to the philosopher, the purpose of human existence lies in the soul's assets and not in external assets or those of the body, even though leisure and fun were necessary for human life. He preached balance and the middle ground as the main characteristics of virtue. The pursuit of knowledge was, according to him, the most pleasurable activity, associating intellect with a type of divine nature of the human (Bittar, 2003). Aristotle also adds that the happy man needs friends, given that practicing virtue would be more difficult for those who experience solitude, because in order to be practiced, virtue depends on the presence of someone to receive it (Bittar, 2003).

1.1 Happiness and Well-Being in Contemporary Psychology Studies

Despite the various concepts of happiness and well-being, these terms are often used together in literature. Diener (2009) mentions three different conceptions of well-being. The first is a more external concept of well-being related to individuals' desirable qualities, which, when practiced, can contribute to their development, even if this does not initially lead to a state of contentment. This would be ideal happiness, a state that is independent of the subject's judgment. It is, rather, one of values and virtues, coming close to the concept of eudaimonia that Aristotle advocated. A second concept would be subjective well-being, which is based on the personal judgment of individuals who evaluate the level of satisfaction with their own lives based on the relationship between positive and negative affections. And finally, the third would be the most common and popular definition of the word happiness, i.e., an emotional state where there is a predominance of pleasurable experiences and positive affections over negative ones. Subjective well-being can be influenced by a series of variables such as personal beliefs, the ways in which the individual interacts with the environment, demographic aspects, income, biological and physiological influences, personality traits and social behaviors, values, purpose, and relationships, among others (Diener & Biwas Diener, 2008; Diener, 2009).

Despite the numerous models and concepts of well-being in literature, eudaimonic theories seem to predominate in most of them (Das et al., 2020). We can thus see that the traditional philosophical concepts of hedonia and eudaimonia have ended up being incorporated into contemporary studies and models of happiness and well-being, both from the Western perspective and in Islamic psychology (Joshanloo & Weijers, 2019). The idea of eudaimonia as a higher pleasure and more lasting happiness means that it stimulates the nobler human capacities that differentiate us from animals. It has values as its fundamental basis, as well as other elements such as authenticity, the pursuit of excellence, purpose and meaning, connection, inspiration, and competence (Huta, 2014). Despite having a broad concept, it is closer to virtuous behavior than to happiness itself, since practicing virtues will not always promote intense positive emotions (Diener, 1984), and in certain situations, it may even go against the individual's will.

On the other hand, as well as being temporary, so-called hedonic pleasures such as sex, food, beauty, power, success, and status can contribute to the emergence of addictions and disorders when misused. Likewise, high or intense levels of happiness can end up being harmful, as they trigger increasing and continuous searches for pleasurable sensations, a pattern that can make some behaviors compulsive (Oishi et al., 2007). For this reason, professionals working in the field of psychology should advise their patients about the meaning of the word happiness and the search for more realistic and healthy possibilities of achieving it.

Diener (1984) explains that one of the essential elements for happiness is the actions the subject takes and not necessarily the end result. Perception is another ally of happiness. Losing, for example, is not always bad. Happiness can be experienced when what was lost was actually bad or harmful to the person. This relativized perception of losses and gains, however, does not always occur at the moment but, over time, depends directly on individuals' ability to discern what is good or bad for their life. Most circumstances that bring happiness are preceded by some difficulty or deprivation. Often, the greater the difficulty or deprivation, the greater the feeling of victory and happiness at the end. The idea that only the satisfaction of human needs can maximize happiness is illusory, given that once total satisfaction has been achieved, it becomes more difficult to repeat the experience, especially if the subject has never faced any kind of deprivation in order to appreciate those achievements. This explains why people who felt the highest levels of joy may be the same ones who have suffered the highest levels of negative emotions (Diener, 1984).

Erroneous or inadequate concepts about happiness can be difficult to deconstruct, especially when they generate unrealistic expectations. Expectations can be largely responsible for a person's happiness or unhappiness due to the repercussions they have on the individual's emotions and behaviors (Ferraz et al., 2007; Sheldon & Lyubomirsky, 2019). Cognition and interpretation of the world are decisive elements for happiness, as are social comparisons. Lyubomirsky (2013) and Diener (1984) point this out as one of the attitudes that most influence subjects' satisfaction with their own lives. The social group itself establishes many parameters of comparison, and it is on this basis that individuals will build their life goals. Satisfaction, which oscillates between normal ambition and greed, differs from the moment when the individual's satisfaction depends more on what the other person has than on what they need to meet their needs. According to the theory of social comparisons, it is not the fact or the event itself that determines happiness, but to whom subjects compare themselves. This simple attitude can destroy or raise a person's level of satisfaction and gratitude. Thus, if individuals compare themselves with people who are more fortunate or "lucky," their level of happiness will decrease, while, on the other hand, if they use those who have less than them as a parameter, this level will be higher and they will feel good about what they have (Diener, 1984; Emmons & Diener, 1985).

In addition to being a singular concept that depends on cognitive, emotional, and behavioral aspects, unlike well-being, happiness can have a more selfish facet where individual satisfaction takes precedence over collective satisfaction (Omais, 2018). Poorly elaborated subjective meanings about happiness and exaggerated or distorted life expectations can result in illness, mental disorders, personal dissatisfaction, and conflicts in relationships (Zuzanek & Zuzanek, 2014). The idealization of happiness, or the so-called myths of happiness, arises when individuals condition their expectations on a certain life change, such as finding their dream partner, a job, an increase in salary, children, etc. Idealizations such as these make individuals hostages to hedonic adaptation, a situation in which high expectations, once achieved, cease to be a novelty and the experience is no longer undergone in the same way or with the same intensity as the first time (Seligman, 2004; Lyubomirsky, 2013).

Taking control of one's own happiness and developing the ability to find gratification and contentment autonomously and independently of external circumstances and social influences also requires profound changes in the individual. Hence, the importance of building resources for a more meaningful life. Csikszentmihalyi (2008) describes pleasure as a human's reflex response and reveals that there is an illusion in society that natural or biological impulses are the ideal way to make decisions about what is good or bad. He explains that, in the individual, control over one's own impulses creates independence from the social environment's influences. For Haidt (2006), happiness is something that lies in the middle ground, not something that can be obtained or achieved directly, as a final goal. It therefore depends on various conditions related to both individuals and the quality of their relationships, their affinity with work, and a relationship with something greater than themselves. He also stresses that the vast majority of people are motivated by moral aspects, hence the importance of the goals individuals set also being aligned with the needs of others around them.

One problem with a number of definitions of well-being is that many individuals may exchange pleasurable choices for others which, although less attractive at first, would be more in line with their purpose and values (Diener et al., 2009). In this case, positive emotions and affects would have less priority than those individuals' goals. This "abdication" of positive emotion only occurs because of the meanings constructed throughout life that influence each person's personal choices. An example of this is religious behavior, which often requires giving up certain pleasures out of respect for God and religious principles. These variables need to be considered when assessing subjective well-being in distinct cultures.

Happiness and well-being are directly linked to the social context and the quality of relationships and interactions among people. Diener et al. (2003) explain that individuals' satisfaction is not always the result of satisfaction with themselves, but rather their relationship with others. As well as the inability to postpone gratification or deal with frustrations, there can be an incompatibility between the pursuit of happiness and well-being, especially in more individualistic cultures where social interaction with friends, family, or other people is not frequent and/or relevant (Ford et al., 2015). Therefore, this satisfaction of the self that guides individualistic societies may not be the same type of satisfaction present in collectivist societies.

In the late 1990s, the positive psychology movement emerged, with the aim of broadening psychology's focus from repairing problems to also investing in studies that focus on human beings' qualities. In order to investigate the elements that can lead individuals to having happier lives, Seligman released his work *Authentic Happiness*, highlighting the importance of studying happiness and explaining the impact of positive emotions on the quality of relationships, health, and work. Seligman (2004) also highlights religion's relationship with happiness, satisfaction, and health, emphasizing its importance in building meaning and hope, especially in the face of adverse situations.

In his book *Flourish*, Seligman replaced the term happiness with the term well-being, a construct made up of various elements that together promote human flourishing. The term "flourish" is a metaphor that opposes "withering," representing individuals who, by taking advantage of the resources within themselves and their environment, are able to open up to the world and mature. Seligman (2011) reports that one of the aims of positive psychology (PP) was to ensure that well-being could provide a more lasting and permanent sense of happiness than the fleeting and temporary sensation provided by hedonic pleasures. The term happiness then became associated with a more subjective and individual perspective, while the concept of well-being encompassed individuals and their social environment. This gave rise to the PERMA model, an acronym that represents the five pillars of well-being: positive emotion, engagement, relationships, meaning, and accomplishment (Seligman, 2011).

1.1.1 Elements of the PERMA Model

The first item in the PERMA acronym is positive emotions. Positive emotions belong to the group of affects, representing consciously accessible and lasting feelings that are the main elements in evaluating subjective well-being and satisfaction with life (Fredrickson, 2001). She lists ten attitudes that arouse positive emotions: joy, fun, gratitude, interest, serenity, hope, admiration, pride, inspiration, and love, which represents the juncture of the other emotions, awakening positive attitudes and behaviors that contribute to the building of social resources in relationships.

It should be noted, however, that in Barbara Fredrickson's (2009) definition, the ten positive emotions cited in her studies do not represent the basic human emotions from a neurological point of view, but rather forms of positivity that generate these emotions. In fact, to this day, the definition of emotion still does not seem very clear, and the way the term is used in positive psychology, for example, differs from the concept of emotion in neuroscience. Ekman (1999) explains that there are various emotions that derive from basic emotions, and they can be related to mood, attitudes, traits, or disorders.

Neuroscience studies, especially those focused on neurophysiology, have shown a wide range of favorable results from positive emotions, both mentally and physically. A simple smile can promote cognitive changes, greater flexibility in attention, a wider range of information processing, and the strengthening of social and family ties (Friedrickson, 1998). Positive emotions expand the field of vision, perception, and attention, as well as relational resources such as connection and inclusion, generating a more expansive and relaxed physical posture (Friedrickson, 2013). In addition, they encourage people to be more open, both mentally and emotionally. This makes people more creative and receptive, encouraging them to build new skills, create stronger emotional bonds, and open up to new knowledge and cultures, as well as improve physical, social, intellectual, and psychological resources. At the same time, Friedrickson (2009) does not deny the importance of negative emotions for human flourishing, emphasizing that it is not humanly possible to live an exclusively positive life.

Among positive emotions, joy is perhaps the one most popularly associated with happiness. Fredrickson (1998) explains that joy is a high-arousal emotion that arises in situations of security, requires little effort, and is generally associated with pleasure. On the other hand, unlike joy, contentment is a low-arousal emotion, marked by a feeling of tranquility and generally present in situations of certainty and confidence that result from the individual's broad view of the world. An interesting point made by Fredrickson (2013) is the distinction between positive emotions and physical pleasures. According to her, when focusing on a physical/corporal desire, the individual's attention is reduced in relation to other objects, unlike the positive emotions researched by the author, which take on more transcendental and abstract characteristics. These data converge with the ideas of hedonism and eudaimonism, which contrast the fleeting and temporary pleasure of the physical and material world with lasting happiness, connected to purposes, values, and virtues.

The second item in the PERMA model is engagement, which is a term related to Csikszentmihalyi's (2008) studies on flow, a state characterized by deep involvement in activities that require a high level of attention and energy from the individual because they are intrinsically rewarding. These activities generate gratification for their own sake, not just for the expected end result. The author points out that the source of happiness is not pleasure but the contentment provided by fulfilling activities that require attention and effort and that generate some personal growth and evolution. For the subject to flow, the activity must include challenges that are proportionate to the individual's ability.

The practice of virtues would be one of these fulfilling activities that generate positive emotions and energize the individual. It was based on this observation that Peterson and Seligman (2004) conducted an extensive study in various countries throughout the world, with the aim of identifying the human qualities most valued around the world in the most diverse cultures and religions. Virtues are characteristics that are valued in the most varied cultures, philosophies, and religions, while character strengths would be instruments for achieving them. The *Values in Action Classification of Character Strengths and Virtues (VIA)* arises from the data collected, covering a list of 24 character strengths, divided and categorized into a group of six virtues: wisdom (creativity, curiosity, open-mindedness, love of learning, perspective); courage (honesty, bravery, persistence, zest); justice (fairness, leadership, teamwork); humanity (kindness, love, social intelligence); temperance (forgiveness, modesty, prudence, self-regulation); and transcendence (appreciation of beauty and excellence, gratitude, hope, humor, and religiousness) (Niemiec, 2019).

The study of human strengths and virtues has become one of the most researched topics in positive psychology. It is also a promising element in the prevention of certain mental illnesses, because character strengths can act as a type of protection against adverse situations. Niemiec (2019) explains that, while the use of strengths favors individuals' state of awareness about themselves, their reality, and their qualities, putting them into practice can also help prevent negative experiences or help interpret life's problems from other perspectives, thus contributing to the process of resilience and recovery in the face of adversity. According to Seligman and Csikszentmihalyi (2000), understanding strengths such as courage, optimism, hope, faith, forgiveness, and more can be determining elements for healthy behavior in individuals.

Although strengths are considered to be constant and stable traits in an individual's personality, it is believed that they can be innate or developed over time in specific situations such as changes in social role, practicing new habits, or as a result of therapeutic interventions (Niemiec, 2019). They are characteristics that, morally, are highly desired and encouraged in young people, families, work environments, and relationships both individually and socially in general, and they help in the individual's personal development and growth (Park & Peterson, 2009).

The third element listed by Seligman (2011) in the PERMA model is relationships, be they love relationships, family relationships, or social relationships in general. The quality of relationships, whether at home or in the workplace, influences not only individuals' moods but also their productivity, their actions, and even their physical health. Although many people think that good relationships make people happier, studies show the opposite, i.e., happy people with higher levels of life satisfaction end up having better family and friendship relationships, as it is natural for people to prefer to connect with those who have a more positive attitude toward life (Diener & Biwas-Diener, 2008). People who are more satisfied and happier end up being more pleasant, enthusiastic, funny, sociable, and attractive than people who are more apathetic or who frequently complain about life.

In the workplace, interpersonal relationships have a direct impact on productivity and enthusiasm related to carrying out tasks. Although different types of relationships are important, those where there is more intimacy seem to have a greater influence on happiness, as they generate a state of security, mutual understanding, support in difficult times, validation, affection, complicity, sexual intimacy, and emotional maturity. Attitudes such as partner appreciation, more positive communication styles, validation, mutual respect, humor, showing affection, compassion, and breaking the daily routine are just a few examples that can favor these relationships (Diener & Biwas-Diener, 2008; Lyubomirsky, 2013).

Sense and Meaning constitute the fourth pillar of Seligman's model. They represent the source of motivation in human life, which is subjectively constructed. There are an infinite number of meanings that human beings can create, and each context will create its own particular senses and meanings. For this reason, studies on sense and meaning in Positive Psychology range from issues related to religiosity and spirituality to the search for meaning in work environments and organizations.

It is important to remember that the tripartite model Diener suggested (1984) points to two elements related to well-being: a cognitive element related to individuals' assessment of their lives and an emotional one that depends on the frequency of positive and negative emotions they experience in their daily lives. The latter element is more objective than the former, so the subjective factor would be cognition and the way of interpreting life's circumstances. While affections encompass feelings, experiences, and emotional states, satisfaction depends on individuals' assessment of life based on their expectations, worldview, and values. Thus, cultural and religious elements can influence cognitive judgment (Das et al., 2020). Cognition has a fundamental influence on this process, moderating emotions and the way a person reacts to events. Thus, culture can have an important influence on this process. According to Feist et al. (1995), it is individuals' minds that determine happiness and direct their emotional state based on their judgment of the experience and not the empirical sensation in isolation. In this case, regardless of whether the event is positive or negative, it is cognition that determines its interpretation. This explains why the meaning of life is a strong predictor of happiness. A study by Jebb et al. (2020) even showed that the strongest associations identified in three measures of subjective well-being in all the world's different regions and in all age groups were those related to the meaning of life.

The objective of life's meaning is often to fill humans' existential emptiness and, according to Frankl (2016), it can be found through work or action, through experiences or people, or even through the attitude toward pain and suffering. Steger (2009) also states that the meaning of life arises through an understanding of individuals' existence, as well as the realization of goals that fill their life. These goals can be found in relationships, justice, self-transcendence, self-acceptance, fulfillment, or religiosity/spirituality. It is these objectives that will direct the goals individuals seek to achieve, acting as intrinsic motivators that drive them toward the realization of plans, actions, goals, and purposes. This cognitive element of meaning stimulates self-reflection, a sense of responsibility, and moral discernment about what is good or bad (Wong, 2012).

The concept of meaning, in simplified terms, is nothing more than the connection and subjective representation of relationships among things or events in life

(Baumeister, 1991). As cognitive elements, they build mental representations that help individuals understand the connections among life's various elements. According to Martela and Steger (2016), there are three elements related to meaning. The first, coherence, is a cognitive element responsible for constructing a representational scheme with connected information that helps the subject understand the logic of life, such as religious doctrines or philosophies and their content. The second purpose represents the motivational element that drives the construction and execution of goals that will guide individuals' actions based on their values, thus excluding objectives that are not in line with these elements. And finally, the third would be significance, an element of an evaluative nature responsible for building a value about life, a life worth living. Purpose is directly connected to significance because persisting with certain objectives requires a motivation that needs to be linked to very strong and relevant values. In this way, coherence serves to provide clarity and mentally organize the information that will trigger the building of purpose and significance (Martela & Steger, 2016).

PERMA's fifth pillar is linked to accomplishment, to the search for a fulfilling life, the gratification of which results from one or more achieved goals. When interconnected, certain factors such as setting goals and objectives, optimism, determination, self-efficacy, and a growth mindset, among others, can help people achieve what they want. Achievement is proportional to the level of effort expended, i.e., the greater the time invested in a given activity, the greater the feeling of achievement and victory. It is not always sought for pleasure or for its meaning but simply for its own sake, without coercion (Seligman, 2011). On the other hand, a study carried out by Goh et al. (2021) to identify how PERMA's elements relate to each other proved that achievement is influenced considerably by meaning, which acts as an intrinsic motivation driving the individual to achieve.

Optimism is considered a fundamental concept for fulfillment. The way people think about their problems influences the types of emotions they feel. A pessimistic explanatory style leads to momentary feelings of discouragement and helplessness which, if prolonged, can lead to depression. Pessimists tend to see problems as something exclusively linked to them and not to other variables, believing that their effects are permanent and eternal, with no possibility of change. They take fewer risks and abandon their goals and ambitions. Contrary to the pessimist's defeatist view, optimistic individuals see life's setbacks as challenges. They do not attribute causes solely to themselves but also to other circumstances, seeing them as occasional situations. This way of thinking allows for a more proactive recovery and coping with the situation. This, in turn, makes individuals persist longer in their goals, even in the face of obstacles, which explains why optimistic people tend to maintain healthy habits in the long term, adhere to medical treatments, and have greater longevity (Seligman, 2005). The relationship between optimism and resilience results in a better ability to cope, especially in situations of despair, anguish, and distress.

Although PERMA is a very widespread model in positive psychology, we must note that it is not the only one and does not encompass all the elements of well-being. Several other models have included different elements in their structures, such as health, career, finance, resilience, culture, sustainability, and others (Kern, 2022; Turner et al., 2017). This shows that positive psychology is a field of study that is constantly growing, with increasingly holistic and comprehensive models related to well-being.

1.2 Positive Psychology's Different Waves and the Need for a Decolonial Perspective in Well-Being Research

Positive psychology is an evolving movement whose trajectory has been traced in a very short space of time. We must therefore understand the fluid and dynamic process it has gone through over the years. The emergence of PP's first wave inaugurated the idea of studying the factors that would enable the "optimal" and positive functioning of human beings, positive emotions, and interventions that could maximize individuals' talents and qualities. In reality, we cannot say that Positive Psychology has brought about a "new" field of study, but rather that it has rescued, compiled, organized, and repaginated an object of investigation that, somewhat dispersed and dormant, already existed in psychological literature.

Over time, a second wave emerged, with the aim of including not only the study of positive emotions but also the dialectical and dichotomous relationship among different emotions and their impact on well-being (Wong, 2011; Lomas & Ivtzan, 2015). PP's second wave reinforced the need for balance in order to achieve human flourishing, including the adaptations and transformations that adverse situations and negative emotions can cause in people's lives and how this can lead to flourishing (Lomas, 2016). Thus, just as optimism can stimulate strengths like perseverance, pessimism can encourage prudence, while anger can feed the spirit of struggle and justice. Similarly, just as serenity favors decision-making and the creative process, anger can be of great importance in the search for change and social movements (Lomas & Ivtzan, 2015).

After this second stage, a new wave emerged in PP, proposed by Wissing (2018). She questioned some of the first and second waves' limitations and studies in the area's excessive focus on Western values that are not always appropriate for other peoples. This third wave's objective would be to encompass other fields of knowledge besides psychology, as well as different experiences, concepts, and paradigms of well-being present in different cultures, religions, and social groups through interdisciplinary, multidisciplinary, and transdisciplinary study perspectives. Thus, instead of focusing specifically on the individual, a broader and more integrated paradigm is sought that includes cultural, political, spiritual/religious, environmental, and social influences in general. Different religions, for example, can produce different results when it comes to well-being. Studies focused on evaluating and comparing these differences are still rare in the literature.

This new idea opens the door for concepts of happiness to be explored in science not through the lens of a single culture, as has been the case for so long, but rather for other worldviews to be incorporated into the study of well-being (Lomas et al., 2020). This proposal also opens up space for new methodologies and epistemologies beyond those that were already being used in the first wave, as well as for the study of standardizations and requirements that establish the ethical limits of action in this area. Also noteworthy is the convergence of this movement with indigenous psychology and decolonial theories, with the aim of adding epistemologies aligned with the values, beliefs, and traditions of non-Western cultures to the scientific repertoire (Omais & Santos, 2024).

Considering that most studies on well-being are carried out by researchers from the USA (Das et al., 2020), the constructs and conceptual models will certainly be based on values linked to this cultural perspective, such as autonomy, self-determination, self-esteem, and other elements more related to the individual. This begs the question: is it really possible to gauge accurate results on well-being in other societies using instruments built from the cultural perspective of a single country or geographical region? Despite science's efforts to broaden this horizon, can we say that studies constructed over decades under this single cultural vision can serve as an accurate reference for researching other peoples and cultures? And how can this be reconciled when mental health care involves religious beliefs? In this case specifically, Agilkaya-Sahin (2024, p. 153) affirms that "essential components of the cultural, religious and spiritual aspects should be considered in Positive Psychology." The use of conventional parameters and predictors of happiness universalizes and imposes, directly or indirectly, standards of well-being that are not always suitable for all peoples. For this reason, decoloniality has gained a prominent role as perhaps one of the greatest revolutions in science in recent times, after decades of centralized studies focused on exclusively Western values. At this point, the third wave of positive psychology is shaping up as a major advance, opening up space for a science of happiness and well-being that includes human diversity.

References

Agilkaya-Sahin, Z. (2024). The compatibility of positive psychology for pastoral care and counseling. In S. Bulut (Ed.), *Positive psychology in daily life*, 2024 Ed. (pp. 126–161). Global Books Organisation.

Aristóteles. (2003). *Ética a Nicômaco*. Martin Claret.

Baumeister, R. F. (1991). *Meanings of life*. Guilford Press.

Bittar, E. C. B. (2003). *Curso de Filosofia Aristotélica: Leitura e Interpretação do Pensamento Aristotélico*. Manole.

Csikszentmihalyi, M. (2008). *Flow: The psychology of optimal experience*. Harper Perennial Modern Classics.

Das, K. V., Jones-Harrell, C., Fan, Y., Ramaswami, A., Orlove, B., & Botchwey, N. (2020). Understanding subjective well-being: Perspectives from psychology and public health. *Public Health Reviews, 41*(1). https://doi.org/10.1186/s40985-020-00142-5

Diener, E., & Biwas-Diener, R. (2008). *Happiness: Unlocking the mysteries of psychological wealth*. Blackwell.

Diener, E. (1984). Subjective well-being. *Psychological Bulletin, 95*(3), 542–575. https://doi.org/10.1037/0033-2909.95.3.542

Diener, E. (2009). *Subjective well-being*. In E. Diener (Ed.), *The science of well-being*. Springer.

Diener, E., Napa Scollon, C., & Lucas, R. E. (2009). The evolving concept of subjective well-being: The multifaceted nature of happiness. *Assessing Well-Being, 67*–100. https://doi.org/10.1007/978-90-481-2354-4_4

Diener, E., Oishi, S., & Lucas, R. E. (2003). Personality, culture, and subjective well-being: Emotional and cognitive evaluations of life. *Annual Review of Psychology, 54*(1), 403–425. https://doi.org/10.1146/annurev.psych.54.101601.145056

Ekman, P. (1999). Basic Emotions. *Handbook of Cognition and Emotion, 45*–60. https://doi.org/10.1002/0470013494.ch3

Emmons, R. A., & Diener, E. (1985). Factors predicting satisfaction judgments: A comparative examination. *Social Indicators Research, 16*(2), 157–167. https://doi.org/10.1007/bf00574615

Feist, G. J., Bodner, T. E., Jacobs, J. F., Miles, M., & Tan, V. (1995). Integrating top-down and bottom-up structural models of subjective well-being: A longitudinal investigation. *Journal of Personality and Social Psychology, 68*(1), 138–150. https://doi.org/10.1037/0022-3514.68.1.138

Ferraz, R. B., Tavares, H., & Zilberman, M. L. (2007). Felicidade: uma Revisão. *Archives of Clinical Psychiatry, 34*(5), 234–242. https://doi.org/10.1590/s0101-60832007000500005

Ford, B. Q., Dmitrieva, J. O., Heller, D., Chentsova-Dutton, Y., Grossmann, I., Tamir, M., Uchida, Y., Koopmann-Holm, B., Floerke, V. A., Uhrig, M., Bokhan, T., & Mauss, I. B. (2015). Culture shapes whether the pursuit of happiness predicts higher or lower well-being. *Journal of Experimental Psychology. General, 144*(6), 1053–1062. https://doi.org/10.1037/xge0000108

Frankl, V. E. (2016). *Em Busca de Sentido: Um Psicólogo no Campo de Concentração*. Vozes.

Fredrickson, B. L. (1998). What good are positive emotions? *Review of General Psychology, 2*(3), 300–319. https://doi.org/10.1037/1089-2680.2.3.300

Fredrickson, B. L. (2001). The role of positive emotions in positive psychology: The broaden-and-build theory of positive emotions. *American Psychologist, 56*(3), 218–226. https://doi.org/10.1037//0003-066x.56.3.218

Fredrickson, B. L. (2009). *Positividade*. Rocco.

Fredrickson, B. L. (2013). Positive emotions broaden and build. In P. Devine & A. Plant (Eds.), *Advances in experimental social psychology* (Vol. v. 47, pp. 1–53). Academic Press. https://doi.org/10.1016/B978-0-12-407236-7.00001-2

Goh, P. S., Goh, Y. W., Jeevanandam, L., Nyolczas, Z., Kun, A., Watanabe, Y., Noro, I., Wang, R., & Jiang, J. (2021). Be happy to be successful: A mediational model of PERMA variables. *Asia Pacific Journal of Human Resources, 60*(3), 632–657. https://doi.org/10.1111/1744-7941.12283

Haidt, J. (2006). *The happiness hypothesis*. Basic Books.

Huta, V. (2014). Eudaimonia. In S. A. David, I. Boniwell, & C. A. Amanda (Eds.), *The Oxford handbook of happiness* (pp. 201–213). Oxford University Press.

Jebb, A. T., Morrison, M., Tay, L., & Diener, E. (2020). Subjective well-being around the world: Trends and predictors across the life span. *Psychology Science, 31*(3), 293–305. https://doi.org/10.1177/0956797619898826

Joshanloo, M., & Weijers, D. (2019). Islamic perspectives on wellbeing. In L. Lambert & N. Pasha-Zaidi (Eds.), *Positive psychology in the Middle East/North Africa*. Springer. https://doi.org/10.1007/978-3-030-13921-6_11

Kern, M. L. (2022). PERMAH: A useful model for focusing on well-being in schools. In K.-A. Allen, M. J. Furlong, D. Vella-Brodrick, & S. M. Suldo (Eds.), *Handbook of positive psychology in schools: Supporting process and practice* (3rd ed., pp. 12–24). Routledge. https://doi.org/10.4324/9781003013778-3

Lomas, T. (2016). Flourishing as a dialectical balance: Emerging insights from second-wave positive psychology. *Palgrave Communications, 2*(1). https://doi.org/10.1057/palcomms.2016.18

Lomas, T., & Ivtzan, I. (2015). Second wave positive psychology: Exploring the positive–negative dialectics of wellbeing. *Journal of Happiness Studies, 17*(4), 1753–1768. https://doi.org/10.1007/s10902-015-9668-y

Lomas, T., Waters, L., Williams, P., Oades, L. G., & Kern, M. L. (2020). Third wave positive psychology: Broadening towards complexity. *The Journal of Positive Psychology, 16*(5), 660–674. https://doi.org/10.1080/17439760.2020.1805501

Lyubomirsky, S. (2013). *Os Mitos Da Felicidade: O Que Deveria Fazer Você Feliz, as Não Faz; O Que Não Deveria Fazer Você Feliz, Mas Faz*. Odisseia.

Martela, F., & Steger, M. F. (2016). The three meanings of meaning in life: Distinguishing coherence, purpose, and significance. *The Journal of Positive Psychology, 11*(5), 531–545. https://doi.org/10.1080/17439760.2015.1137623

Niemiec, R. M. (2019). *Character strengths interventions: A field guide for practitioners*. Hogrefe Publishing.

Oishi, S., Diener, E., & Lucas, R. E. (2007). The optimum level of well-being: Can people be too happy? *Perspectives on Psychological Science, 2*(4), 346–360.

Omais, S. (2018). *Manual de Psicologia Positiva*. Qualitymark.

Omais, S., & dos Santos, M. A. (2024). Psicologia Islâmica: Uma Perspectiva Inclusiva de Epistemologias Religiosas no Campo da Psicologia da Religião. *Psicologia USP, 35*, e220015. https://doi.org/10.1590/0103-6564e220015

Online Etymology Dictionary. (2024). Happiness. Etymonline. https://www.etymonline.com/columns/post/bio

Park, N., & Peterson, C. (2009). Character strengths: Research and practice. *Journal of College and Character, 10*(4). https://doi.org/10.2202/1940-1639.1042

Peterson, C., & Seligman, M. E. P. (2004). *Character strengths and virtues*. Oxford University Press.

Seligman, M. E. P. (2004). *Felicidade Autêntica*. Objetiva.

Seligman, M. E. P. (2005). *Aprenda a Ser Otimista*. Nova Era.

Seligman, M. E. P., & Csikszentmihalyi, M. (2000). Positive psychology: An introduction. *American Psychologist, 55*(1), 5–14. https://doi.org/10.1037/0003-066x.55.1.5

Seligman, M. E. P. (2011). *Florescer: uma Nova Compreensão Sobre a Natureza da Felicidade e do Bem-Estar*. Objetiva.

Sheldon, K. M., & Lyubomirsky, S. (2019). Revisiting the sustainable happiness model and pie chart: Can happiness be successfully pursued? *The Journal of Positive Psychology, 16*(2), 145–154. https://doi.org/10.1080/17439760.2019.1689421

Steger, M. (2009). Meaning in life. In S. J. Lopez, & C. R. Snyder (eds) *The Oxford handbook of positive psychology*. Oxford University Press.

Turner, M., Scott-Young, C. M., & Holdsworth, S. (2017). Promoting wellbeing at university: The role of resilience for students of the built environment. *Construction Management and Economics, 35*(11–12), 707–718. https://doi.org/10.1080/01446193.2017.1353698

Wissing, M. P. (2018). Embracing well-being in diverse contexts: The third wave of positive psychology. In *Invited Address at the First Africa Positive Psychology Conference, Potchefstroom, South Africa*. FAPPC.

Wong, P. T. P. (2011). Positive psychology 2.0: Towards a balanced interactive model of the good life. *Canadian Psychology/Psychologie Canadienne, 52*(2), 69–81. https://doi.org/10.1037/a0022511

Wong, P. T. P. (2012). Toward a dual-systems model of what makes life worth living. In P. T. P. Wong (Ed.), *The human quest for meaning: Theories, research, and applications* (2nd ed., pp. 3–22). Routledge/Taylor & Francis Group.

Zuzanek, J., & Zuzanek, T. (2014). Of happiness and of despair, is there a measure? Time use and subjective well-being. *Journal of Happiness Studies, 16*(4), 839–856. https://doi.org/10.1007/s10902-014-9536-1

Chapter 2
Spirituality, Religiosity, and Well-Being

Spirituality has been incorporated by the World Health Organization (WHO) as one of the elements related to the concept of health. Over time, given the impossibility of disregarding the importance of the spiritual dimension, new terms have emerged to express it. The word spirituality has acquired a more neutral and secular connotation, gaining more acceptance in the scientific environment, serving the most diverse beliefs and groups, including atheists and/or agnostics. On the other hand, religion, its dogmas, and content as such have been more timidly included in studies on mental health and well-being. According to Sisemore (2016), the tension that exists between these concepts is reinforced by a certain rejection of religious institutions that still exists, restricting transcendental expressions to more private contexts.

Although there is no separation between religiosity and spirituality in Islam, there has been a long discussion in Western literature about the concepts, characteristics, similarities, and differences between these two terms. While religion is understood as a structured set of dogmas and beliefs that prescribes practices, rituals, and behaviors, spirituality is seen as the combination of thoughts, feelings, and behaviors resulting from individuals' relationship with the sacred or transcendent, through which they seek answers to internal questions. For Toniol (2017), spirituality is not necessarily something that opposes or contrasts with religion, nor is it linked to it. Therefore, there are no absolute landmarks that clearly differentiate these two dimensions. Pargament et al. (2013) point out that when referring to any relationship that includes both secular and institutional contexts linked to the sacred, using both terms, "spirituality and religiosity," is recommended so that the content is covered more broadly.

According to Koenig (2012, p. 17), there is a link between spirituality and religion due to its connection with the supernatural and the religious language that characterizes it. This is why he emphasizes that "to call something spiritual, there has to be some connection with religion." Hence, he argues that anything not having a connection with religion or the supernatural does not fit into the concept of spirituality but rather into humanism. Thus, positive emotions, values, and the meaning of life, as well as human virtues or any other positive health indicator, according to him, cannot be defined as "spirituality," but rather as a consequence of a spiritual/religious life (Koenig et al., 2024).

2.1   The Positive Effects of Religiosity and Spirituality (R/S) on Mental Health

Despite seeming similar in their general sense, mental health and well-being have certain differences and nuances when it comes to their definitions. Wren-Lewis states that mental health is a type of precondition for achieving well-being and that, although the expanded construct is based on concepts that are very close to those of well-being, there are still important distinctions between the two. The term well-being is linked to a broader concept, associated with a multifactorial perspective, which includes not only the field of mental health or health in general but various other fields of knowledge that are connected to it (Wren-Lewis & Alexandrova, 2021). Thus, mental health is part of the concept of well-being, along with the holistic definition of health established by the World Health Organization.

Paiva (2007) highlights the positive relationship between religion and mental health, remembering that religious precepts or teachings can stimulate healthy behaviors, curb or discourage behaviors that are harmful to individuals or society, encourage social support and community integration, favor coping with adverse situations, and influence individuals' lifestyles. According to Belzen (2009), human emotions themselves can also be influenced by beliefs, desires, and judgments, which, in turn, are constructed through values and customs linked to certain communities.

Religion occupies a place that affects individuals' beliefs about themselves and the world and, due to its precepts and prohibitions, strongly influences individuals' actions and conduct. R/S's multidimensional character encompasses several elements such as beliefs and practices, religious development, spiritual commitment and involvement, religious coping, changes in attitudes, and beliefs about life after death. Studies carried out on people of different age groups, ethnicities, and religions have already identified R/S's positive effects on health, including an increase in the practice of healthy habits and psychological functioning in general. Because of this, Seybold and Peter (2001) reveal the need to understand how much these elements positively influence individuals' functioning. To do so, however, we need to eliminate science's barriers and antagonism in relation to religion so that we may better understand religiosity's and spirituality's contributions to physical and mental health.

Both psychology and religion seek to answer similar questions about life and humanity. At the same time, positive psychology adds to this knowledge by focusing on behaviors and actions that generate positive emotional states. According to Ciarrocchi (2012), spirituality or the feeling of closeness to God can influence subjective well-being and other positive characteristics, although these characteristics are also related to the subject's personality. For this reason, much of the literature on the psychology of religion can be incorporated into positive psychology in a significant way. The author reveals that in some religious systems, religiosity and spirituality end up unifying human virtues in order to achieve happiness. Authors such as Joseph et al. (2007) explain that possible explanations for the relationship between R/S and happiness may lie in the roles established in social relationships and life's purpose. This relationship converges with the results found by Khaw and Kern (2015), confirming that religiosity and spirituality were among the most frequent responses when participants were asked about the meaning of life, happiness, and well-being.

Religiosity and spirituality are important elements in coping with challenging situations and are resources that can enable the construction of new meanings and a feeling of greater security in the face of life events (Sisemore, 2016). According to Ciarrocchi (2012), the benefits linked to religious and/or spiritual practices are mainly an improvement in health and well-being and a reduction in impulsive behaviors such as substance use, criminal behavior, and domestic violence. Diener and Biwas-Diener (2008) state that, in addition to religion being one of the characteristics that most differentiate us from animals, it functions as a kind of mindset, a mentality that influences behaviors and cognition, and helps people feel good about themselves and others. They mention some "active ingredients" that can contribute to happiness and well-being. Among these are social support, a sense of community, beliefs that comfort the individual, a sense of identity and meaning, a family environment where these same religious beliefs can be shared, and moral and ethical teachings.

Religion and culture are among the predictors of subjective well-being. Das et al. (2020) point out that both influence how we interpret experiences as positive or negative. According to the authors, religion can positively influence subjective well-being in various ways, such as in the formulation of goals and objectives, in the construction of one's own definition of well-being and happiness, in the association of values with certain actions or activities, in optimism, in coping with stress and adverse situations, and in some parameters of self-assessment and social comparison. However, it should be noted that well-being resulting from spirituality depends on individuals' focus on religious content. Many people can become attached to the punitive elements of religion, such as guilt, sin, belittlement, and fear of hell or other punishments. For this reason, Diener and Biwas-Diener (2008) warn that the problem is not the belief itself. A person may have a belief, for example, in life after death, which includes the dimensions of Heaven and Hell, but the fact that they restrict their gaze solely to the aspect of Hell, of punishment, instead of perceiving the various possibilities that the belief itself offers, can generate anxiety and other feelings that have a negative impact on levels of well-being.

Positive emotions are not only restricted to good moments in life but are fundamental factors in the process of resilience, providing an improvement in mental flexibility, skills such as problem-solving, and recovery from stressful experiences (Fredrickson & Branigan, 2005). According to Smith et al. (2012), resilience and positive emotions may be two of the most influential factors in health and well-being. The authors point to studies in which spirituality practiced in a healthy way resulted in higher levels of positive emotions and resilience, which is basically due to four elements: relationships, values, personal meanings, and coping. The way we think about an event can affect the emotions linked to that experience (Lazarus & Delongis, 1983). This is why the influence of spirituality on the way an individual thinks about and reframes the events that happen to them has repercussions on the quality of the emotions they experience (Fredrickson, 2002).

There is a very close relationship between coping, religious beliefs and strategies, and resilience. Spirituality and religiosity create opportunities and encourage the individual to cultivate positive emotions, such as gratitude, love, admiration, and serenity, as well as contributing to the formation of more positive meanings for interpreting life events and stressful situations. Spiritual practices and rituals stimulate positive emotions, as do their teachings and philosophy of life. For this reason, authors such as Fredrickson (2002) reveal that not only do spiritual practices themselves provoke a feeling of contentment, but also the teachings related to those practices, such as nonjudgment and acceptance.

In Vaillant's (2010) view, the feeling of trust provided by the word "faith" is a factor that in itself creates an overlap of positive emotions prevailing over negative emotions. He emphasizes that positive emotions such as love, hope, joy, forgiveness, compassion, and gratitude are directly linked to an individual's spirituality, as are other feelings such as respect, appreciation, empathy, tenderness, and acceptance. According to the author, positive emotions would be the path to human evolution, pointing out that over several centuries, religions "have been the best means the community has found to bring positive emotions to conscious reflection" (Vaillant, 2010, p. 18).

We must point out that simply belonging to a particular religion without practicing it does not always confirm religiosity's and spirituality's positive role. The meaning brought about by religious practices, as well as levels of satisfaction with life, are related to the presence of religion in individuals' lives, frequent practice, and the subject's real commitment to it. The results shown by Berthold and Ruch (2014) indicate that people would only benefit from religiosity if they were truly engaged in religious involvement.

The teachings of various world religions, including Islam, are one of the major sources for Peterson and Seligman's study (2004) that gave rise to character strengths. Most religions and religious philosophies place great emphasis on human behavior's ethical and moral attributes, encouraging human evolution and development through the practice of virtues. Religiosity seems to influence levels of well-being directly or indirectly by encouraging attitudes such as the practice of gratitude, kindness, and forgiveness, which provide the subject with considerable emotional relief (Berthold & Ruch, 2014).

Unlike positive psychology, where spirituality is considered an independent force, in Islam, spirituality is the basis of all other forces and virtues. The ethical-moral aspects and the understanding of virtuous conduct as an act of worship in Islam represent a great incentive to practice pro-social behavior (Omais et al., 2023).

This finding converges with a longitudinal study of 1352 adolescents by Kor et al. (2019), which confirmed spirituality's positive influence on prosocial behavior, level of life satisfaction, and quality of emotions. These data show that spirituality is directly related to subjective well-being and prosocial characteristics. The authors also emphasize that spirituality should be a differentiated force, a dimension independent of the other forces, since it alone contributes to the development of the others.

Emotions and relationships are two closely linked dimensions. Most of the frustrations and negative or positive emotions we experience turn out to be the result of the relationships we establish with people. Misunderstandings, indifference, contempt, and envy are attitudes that lead to isolation and, consequently, negative emotions such as anger and sadness (Omais, 2018). Religiosity and spirituality have repercussions on both marital and family life. Child raising by couples with high levels of spirituality, for example, may be associated with higher levels of marital satisfaction (Parker et al., 2011). In the marital sphere, forgiveness, reconciliation, and the restoration of past relationships are often encouraged from a spiritual and religious point of view (Smith et al., 2012). Forgiveness is a fundamental factor for a relationship's longevity and an element strongly present in religions. The absence of forgiveness can lead to rancorous behavior, retaliation, or revenge, attitudes that aggravate conflicts in couples and result in a poorer quality of relationship (David & Stafford, 2013).

The couple's commitment to God involves a pact with a transcendental dimension. This can, in some cases, have a positive influence on the marriage, especially in times of conflict when it is necessary to create new meanings for the relationship (Goulart, 2018). Alves-Silva et al. (2017) state that the influence of religious dogma, the fulfillment of the marital commitment before the community and religious institutions, the sharing of the same faith by the couple, and their relationship with support networks and religious groups in their own community may be some of the factors that contribute to a relationship's longevity. Marital breakdown is generally discouraged or even forbidden in certain religions. Such prohibitions can end up having positive effects on the marriage, as they create a greater sense of responsibility and encourage spouses to look for better and more functional strategies to maintain the relationship (Alves-Silva et al., 2017).

For Thoresen (1999), in addition to reinforcing their beliefs, practices, and experiences, during difficult times people involved in religious or spiritual contexts can also count on the social support of the community or religious organizations in adverse situations, which contributes to the process of coping and resilience. According to him, sociocultural factors combined with a religious context can stimulate not only healthy behaviors but also more positive social behaviors, such as building friendships, giving to others, and practicing love and compassion as life principles, thus reducing individualistic behaviors.

Religions are great sources of meaning in human life. The construction of meaning and significance generates greater confidence in individuals, hence its relationship with well-being. The way meanings are constructed differs between religious and nonreligious individuals. Newton and McIntosh (2013) point to four factors that explain the uniqueness of religions in producing positive meanings. The first factor is comprehensiveness. Religion, compared to other sources of meaning, is broader and deeper in its content because, in addition to the guidance provided regarding beliefs, behaviors, purposes, perceptions, and emotions, it also includes transcendental, existential, and metaphysical explanations that answer many of humans' questions and needs. A second factor is the association of sacredness with meanings, associating individuals' various objectives and purposes with transcendental elements, the divine, values linked to morality, and a future expectation of reward or punishment. So, for example, if someone considers it important to protect animals only for their well-being, adding that protecting them is also a religious duty, or even that treating them badly is a sin and could lead to punishment in the future, could make the meaning more relevant to motivate action. A third factor is the specific beliefs of some religions, such as believing in life after death, the Final Judgment, predestination, and a divine plan that is beyond human comprehension. And finally, the fourth factor covers the social aspect of religions: the sense of community, mutual support and interactions, joint practices, as well as the construction of a generational history around religion that transmits and reinforces religious teachings over time (Newton & McIntosh, 2013).

The creation of senses and meanings from religious and spiritual sources is a fundamental resource in the process of resilience and coping with adverse situations such as crises and family conflicts. From a cognitive point of view, as well as helping people to overcome challenging situations, spirituality provides new perspectives on stressful life experiences, giving them new meaning in various ways (Lazarus & Delongis, 1983). Religiosity influences the interpretation of adverse circumstances through religious attributions, such as the belief that everything will be fine later (hope, optimism). The belief that God is there to provide support and protection (trust, security) is also another example of how such cognitions can bring a greater sense of relief to the individual (Pargament, 1997).

The construction of new meanings through religion can also generate different meanings about pleasure, the main objective of hedonic happiness. When it comes to spirituality and religiosity, there seems to be an inverse relationship between the search for pleasure and the search for meaning and significance. This is an interesting fact, as many religions encourage behaviors that involve a certain renunciation on the human's part in exchange for a greater cause or objective that aligns with the meanings constructed by religiosity itself. Many of these renunciations involve the exchange of pleasures or immediate gratifications of the most diverse kinds, most of which are associated with hedonism, inherently human impulses and desires. To assess the relationship between pleasure, engagement, and meaning, Berthold and Ruch (2014) observed in their study that subjects with higher levels of religiosity obtained lower scores on items related to pleasure, thus showing a negative relationship between religiosity and pleasure, and a positive relationship between religiosity and meaning. This finding converges with the concept of eudaimonic happiness. The meanings given by religion generally favor eudaimonia over hedonia. The exchange of immediate pleasure for its postponement, justified by a greater purpose, is an element constantly reinforced by religions through meanings linked to faith.

An individual's level of attachment to religiosity or spirituality is also closely linked to hope and optimism (Ciarrocchi et al., 2008). Explanatory styles and the way life events are interpreted define whether a person has a more optimistic or pessimistic outlook. While pessimistic individuals tend to see negative events as something internal, stable, and global, generalizing the way things happen, optimistic individuals see negative events as something situational, temporary, and specific, that is, limited to specific life situations (Gillham et al., 2001; Seligman, 2005). Faith also builds a similar vision by orienting the individual that adversities are temporary and part of life, being divine determinations that are not necessarily under an individual's control but can serve as a process of learning, strengthening, and evolution of the subject.

2.2   The Positive Effects of Religiosity and Spirituality (R/S) on Physical Health

An important point to remember that directly influences well-being is physical health, which directly reflects on mental health, just as mental health also reflects on physical health. People who engage in religious services tend to receive greater social support and engage in healthy behaviors, such as exercising and not taking part in risky behaviors like smoking, drinking alcohol, etc. (Park & Slattery, 2012). There are several possible combinations of factors that, together with spirituality and religiosity, can positively affect health, some of which are social support, the incorporation of healthy habits, effects or changes in the individual's own cognition or psychodynamics, cognitive belief systems, religious practices, the use of language to express suffering, and other processes related to health that are not always explained by science (Moreira-Almeida et al., 2006; Thoresen, 1999).

Spirituality can be a protective and health-promoting mechanism. It can affect the brain in ways that promote stress reduction and the production of neurotransmitters linked to positive moods, as well as providing an analgesic effect that reduces the sensation of pain in patients with chronic pain (Jonas et al., 2012). Social support within the community, rules and ways of life focused on ethical and moral conduct and values, and rituals used to reduce stress, such as prayer, meditation, reading books and sacred scriptures, dietary guidelines, and virtuous practices and behaviors such as humility, honesty, charity, hope, and faith become important coping strategies for individuals (Smith et al., 2012).

Religious practices themselves also play an important role in terms of well-being and positive emotions. Neuroimaging studies show activation of specific brain areas during spiritual practices, changes in the activation pattern of brain structures, cognitive states, and the production of hormones such as serotonin and norepinephrine, among others (Beauregard, 2012). Park and Slattery (2012) also report that attitudes such as gratitude, optimism, hope, forgiveness, or compassion can result in a better state of health, better quality of sleep, and greater adherence to health treatments.

The positive outcomes of religiosity and spirituality mentioned throughout this chapter are just a small sample of the numerous benefits of this construct on mental and physical health. This is a vast field of research that can be expanded to various related topics and diverse forms of spirituality and religiosity. Both positive psychology and the psychology of religion, as well as pastoral psychology, share common points that can yield interesting results in the field of mental health and well-being when used together (Agilkaya-Sahin, 2018). Specific studies on Islam, for example, have already demonstrated the beneficial effects of Quran recitation in reducing depression and anxiety (Koenig et al., 2024). However, although research on the mental health and well-being benefits of Islamic R/S has grown significantly in recent years, this field can still be further explored given the richness of practices, rituals, and beliefs that comprise the Islamic religion. Studies such as the one by Tanhan and Jovem (2022) highlight the existence of gaps in the approaches to Muslims in mental health services. These gaps ultimately hinder a deeper understanding of the issues faced by these individuals, their families, and their communities. This is a broad field of study that has been gradually expanding in the scientific literature, particularly with the resurgence of an epistemology more aligned with the values of this population, Islamic psychology, with theories that will be explored in greater depth in the next chapters.

References

Ağılkaya Şahin, Z. (2018). Bridging pastoral psychology and positive psychology. *Ilahiyat Studies – A Journal on Islamic and Religious Studies, 9*(2), 183–210.

Alves-Silva, J. D., Scorsolini-Comin, F., & Santos, M. A. (2017). Bodas para uma Vida: Motivos para Manter um Casamento de Longa Duração. *Temas em Psicologia, 25*(2), 487–501. https://doi.org/10.9788/TP2017.2-05

Beauregard, M. (2012). Neuroimaging and spiritual practice. In L. J. Miller (Ed.), *The Oxford handbook of psychology and spirituality* (pp. 500–513). Oxford University Press.

Belzen, J. A. (2009). Psicologia Cultural da Religião: Perspectivas, Desafios e Possibilidades. *Revista de Estudos da Religião*, 1–29. https://www.pucsp.br/rever/rv4_2009/t_belzen.pdf

Berthold, A., & Ruch, W. (2014). Satisfaction with life and character strengths of non-religious and religious people: It's practicing one's religion that makes the difference. *Frontiers in Psychology, 5*(876). https://doi.org/10.3389/fpsyg.2014.00876

Ciarrocchi, J. W. (2012). A positive psychology and spirituality: A virtue-informed approach to well-being. In L. J. Miller (Ed.), *The Oxford handbook of psychology and spirituality* (pp. 425–436). Oxford University Press.

Ciarrocchi, J. W., Dy-Liacco, G. S., & Deneke, E. (2008). Gods or rituals? Relational faith, spiritual discontent, and religious practices as predictors of hope and optimism. *The Journal of Positive Psychology, 3*(2), 120–136. https://doi.org/10.1080/17439760701760666

Das, K. V., Jones-Harrell, C., Fan, Y., Ramaswami, A., Orlove, B., & Botchwey, N. (2020). Understanding subjective well-being: perspectives from psychology and public health. *Public Health Reviews, 41*(1). https://doi.org/10.1186/s40985-020-00142-5

David, P., & Stafford, L. (2013). A relational approach to religion and spirituality in marriage: The role of couples' religious communication in marital satisfaction. *Journal of Family Issues, 20*(10), 1–18. https://doi.org/10.1177/0192513X13485922

Diener, E., & Biwas-Diener, R. (2008). *Happiness: Unlocking the mysteries of psychological wealth.* Blackwell Publishing.

Fredrickson, B. L. (2002). How does religion benefit health and well-being? Are positive emotions active ingredients? *Psychological Inquiry, 13*(3), 209–213. https://psycnet.apa.org/record/2003-04271-010

Fredrickson, B. L., & Branigan, C. (2005). Positive emotions broaden the scope of attention and thought-action repertoires. *Cognition and Emotion, 19*(3), 313–332. https://doi.org/10.1080/02699930441000238

Gillham, J. E., Shatté, A. J., Reivich, K. J., & Seligman, M. E. P. (2001). Optimism, pessimism, and explanatory style. In E. C. Chang (Ed.), *Optimism & pessimism: Implications for theory, research, and practice* (pp. 53–75). American Psychological Association. https://doi.org/10.1037/10385-003

Goulart, S. A. (2018). *Religiosidade/Espiritualidade em Casamentos de Longa Duração.* 172f. Dissertation. Programa de Pós-Graduação em Psicologia, Universidade Federal do Triângulo Mineiro, Uberaba.

Jonas, W. B., Fritts, M., Christopher, G., Jonas, M., & Jonas, S. (2012). Spirituality, science and the human body. In L. J. Miller (Ed.), *The Oxford handbook of psychology and spirituality* (pp. 361–378). Oxford University Press.

Joseph, S., Linley, P. A., & Maltby, J. (2007). Positive psychology, religion, and spirituality. *Mental Health, Religion & Culture, 9*(3), 209–212. https://doi.org/10.1080/13694670600615227

Khaw, D., & Kern, M. L. (2015). A cross-cultural comparison of the PERMA model of well-being. *Undergraduate Journal of Psychology at Berkeley, 8*, 9–23.

Koenig, H. G. (2012). *Medicina, Religião e Saúde: O Encontro da Ciência e da Espiritualidade* (I. Abreu Trad.). L&PM Editores.

Koenig, H. G., Vanderweele, T. J., & Peteet, J. R. (2024). *Handbook of religion and health* (3rd ed.). Oxford University Press.

Kor, A., Pirutinsky, S., Mikulincer, M., Shoshani, A., & Miller, L. (2019). A longitudinal study of spirituality, character strengths, subjective well-being, and prosociality in middle school adolescents. *Frontiers in Psychology, 10*, 377. https://doi.org/10.3389/fpsyg.2019.00377

Lazarus, R. S., & DeLongis, A. (1983). Psychological stress and coping in aging. *American Psychologist, 38*(3), 245–254. https://doi.org/10.1037/0003-066X.38.3.245

Moreira-Almeida, A., Lotufo Neto, F., & Koenig, H. G. (2006). Religiousness and mental health: A review. *Brazilian Journal of Psychiatry, 28*(3), 242–250.

Newton, T., & McIntosh, D. N. (2013). Unique contributions of religion to meaning. *The Experience of Meaning in Life*, 257–269. https://doi.org/10.1007/978-94-007-6527-6_20

Omais, S. (2018). *Manual de Psicologia Positiva.* Qualitymark.

Omais, S., Tarif, E., & Santos, M. A. (2023). Ethics, morals, virtues and character strengths: A comparison between Islamic psychology and positive psychology. In C. Y. Al-Karam (Ed.), *The way of love* (pp. 129–152). Al Karam Press.

Paiva, G. J. (2007). Religião, Enfrentamento e Cura: Perspectivas Psicológicas. *Estudos de Psicologia, 24*(1), 99–104. https://doi.org/10.1590/s0103-166x2007000100011

Pargament, K. I. (1997). *The psychology of religion and coping.* The Guilford Press.

Pargament, K. I., Exline, J. J., & Jones, J. W. (Eds.). (2013). *APA handbook of psychology, religion, and spirituality (Vol. 1): Context, theory, and research.* American Psychological Association. https://doi.org/10.1037/14045-000

Park, C. L., & Slattery, J. M. (2012). Spirituality, emotions, and physical health. In *The Oxford handbook of positive psychology and spirituality* (pp. 379–387). Oxford University Press.

Parker, J. A., Mandleco, B., Olsen, R. S., Freeborn, D., & Dyches, T. T. (2011). Religiosity, spirituality, and marital relationships of parents raising a typically developing child or a child with a disability. *Journal of Family Nursing, 17*(1), 82–104. https://doi.org/10.1177/1074840710394856

Peterson, C., & Seligman, M. E. P. (2004). *Character strengths and virtues*. Oxford University Press.

Seligman, M. E. P. (2005). *Aprenda a ser otimista*. Nova Era.

Seybold, K. S., & Peter, C. (2001). The role of religion and spirituality in mental and physical health. *American Psychological Society, 10*(1), 21–24. https://doi.org/10.1097/YCO.0000000000000080

Sisemore, S. (2016). *The psychology of religion and spirituality: From the inside out*. Wiley.

Smith, B. W., Ortiz, J. A., Wiggins, K. T., Bernard, J. F., & Dalen, J. (2012). Spirituality, resilience, and positive emotions. In *The Oxford handbook of psychology and spirituality* (pp. 437–454). Oxford University Press.

Tanhan, A., & Young, J. S. (2022). Muslims and mental health services: A concept map and a theoretical framework. *Journal of Religion and Health, 61*, 23–63. https://doi.org/10.1007/s10943-021-01324-4

Thoresen, C. E. (1999). Spirituality and health: Is there a relationship? *Journal of Health Psychology, 4*(3), 291–300. https://doi.org/10.1177/135910539900400314

Toniol, R. (2017). O Que Faz a Espiritualidade? *Religião e Sociedade, 37*, 144–175. https://doi.org/10.1590/0100-85872017v37n2cap06

Vaillant, G. E. (2010). *Fé: Evidências Científicas*. Manole.

Wren-Lewis, S., & Alexandrova, A. (2021). Mental health without well-being. *Journal of Medicine and Philosophy, 46*(6), 684–703. https://doi.org/10.1093/jmp/jhab032

Chapter 3
The Concepts of Happiness in Islamic Philosophy

The Middle Ages in the Western world were marked by the insertion of religion into philosophical thought. The European scenario in the medieval era generated a series of confrontations, thus creating a strong rejection of the presence of religious ideas in science. For this reason, the study of happiness under religious paradigms is not always well received, especially in psychological science, where there is still resistance and even a certain disbelief regarding these epistemologies. In Islam, there were no barriers to science or the search for knowledge. Unlike the medieval context, Islamic teachings unite religion with science, believing that it is through knowledge, contemplation, and observation of the magnitude of creation that human beings will be able to perceive the greatness of God.

3.1 Happiness in Islamic Philosophy

One of the pioneering Muslim scholars writing about happiness from an Islamic perspective, as well as one of the forerunners of translations of Greek works, was Abū Yūsuf Yaʻqūb ibn 'Isḥāq aṣ-Ṣabbāḥ Al-Kindi. With a considerable output of approximately 231 works, 5 of them specifically on psychology, Al-Kindi emphasized that the spirit of knowledge, regardless of the type of knowledge, should have truth as its sole end, as in religious teachings. He did not criticize the pursuit of pleasure but warned that excessive involvement in it could generate affliction, pain, and unhappiness for the soul, emphasizing that the intellectual faculties would be the true direction toward virtue and happiness (Attie Filho, 2002).

In Al-Kindi's view, happiness could be sought in earthly life and in the afterlife (Attie Filho, 2002). In order to deal with the losses and frustrations of life and avoid feelings of sadness, individuals would need to develop the ability to adapt well. For this reason, he argues that just knowing the path to happiness is not enough, but one must also understand the elements that can make an individual unhappy. Concerns

S. Omais, *Happiness and Well-Being in Islam*, https://doi.org/10.1007/978-3-031-95353-8_3

about material possessions or the fear of losing them at any time would be obstacles to achieving contentment. Sadness, according to this philosopher, is a passing emotion. It is an emotional state that can be created, anticipated, or prolonged over time by individuals themselves, and it is precisely the relationship between the emotion and time, and not the event itself, that makes people unhappy. This is why happiness and spiritual contentment should be a habit, an acquired trait, just like virtues, which also become habits over time, making it easier to cope with adversity.

Abu Zayd Al-Balkhi, a polymath with more than 60 books and manuscripts in various areas of knowledge, including psychology, also left significant intellectual output and reflections about happiness. He was one of the pioneers in including mental health in medical science, as well as one of the first scholars to differentiate between mental and psychological disorders and to suggest cognitive-behavioral techniques long before we had this modality in modern psychological theories (Badri, 2013; Raudah et al., 2023).

Al-Balkhi pointed out that it was not possible to live a worldly life free from fear and sadness, as real happiness would only exist in the afterlife. However, he recommended that individuals enjoy the good things in life with contentment and satisfaction, valuing their friends' company and stimulating activities. Through his cognitive-behavioral studies, he developed the idea that emotional states are a consequence of thoughts. For him, happiness would be the root of all positive emotional states such as tranquility and joy. His description of happiness includes its opposites, that is, sadness, despair, and everything that prevents an individual from being happy. One of the strategies the philosopher suggests, for example, to reduce emotional impact in situations of loss is for the individual to reflect on worse situations that could have happened to them but, however, had not (Badri, 2013).

Al-Farabi's and Ibn Miskawayh's works made significant contributions to the philosophical study of happiness. Al-Farabi's writings reveal the influence of Aristotelian studies, and among the more than 100 works he wrote, *Tahsil al-Sa'adah* and *Kitab al-Tanbih'ala Sabil al-As'adah* stand out, among others. For Al-Farabi, the purpose of all human faculties is the pursuit of happiness. According to him, there is nothing greater that an individual can achieve in life. This concept of happiness is marked by the collective concept, the concept of the city, where actions, skills, and abilities converge in order to achieve the happiness of all souls. He emphasized the social aspect and the importance of people forming groups with similarities, so that everyone can share their experiences, difficulties, fears, and pleasures, as well as their goods and food (Awaad et al., 2021). He broadens the concept of happiness from the micro to the macro, that is, from the individual to society, linking it to politics and social elements. Politics, for him, represented the virtuous city and was metaphorically compared to the body's organs, which, in order to achieve full, healthy, and harmonious physical functioning, need to have a common purpose. This conception resembles one of the Prophet Muhammad's sayings (ﷺ): "The believers in their mutual kindness, compassion, and sympathy are just like one body. When one of the limbs suffers, the whole body responds to it with wakefulness and fever" (Bukhârî and Muslim).

Al-Farabi associates human happiness, at its highest level, with elements such as good behavior and manners (*akhlaq*) shaped by a good upbringing (*adab*), a strong intellect, morality, and human qualities, which are evidenced through conduct and actions. The philosopher mentions four aspects that contribute to an individual's contentment: intellectual virtues, theoretical virtues, ethical virtues, and the practice of art. Virtues would be shaped by spirituality so that, from a balance between body and soul, the individual could achieve a state of happiness. He uses the same logic as diseases of the body to explain diseases of the soul. The soul's health depends on education, life goals, good deeds, and ethics, while the main cause of disease of the soul is bad behavior, the effects of which have repercussions on individuals and their bodies. Although bad actions may seem satisfying at the time, in the long run they generate suffering, unlike the good things in life that seem difficult at first but, after a while, generate real contentment. It is difficult to distinguish between good and bad, since often what we see as good becomes bad, and what seems bad becomes something good (Iskakuly et al., 2021). This reasoning also converges with the Quranic verse, "Perhaps you dislike something which is good for you and like something which is bad for you. Allah knows and you do not know" (The Clear Quran, n.d. 2:216).

Happiness is not something static but rather a goal to be achieved. Thus, this philosopher does not restrict the search for happiness to the world of contemplation or philosophy alone but encourages the union of knowledge with action. Al-Farabi argues that real happiness cannot be achieved in worldly life. This is because happiness is the pursuit of perfection, and if both the human being and worldly life are imperfect by nature, then there would be no way to achieve a state of real and perfect happiness if perfection does not exist in this context. Worldly happiness will always be imperfect, temporary, and incomplete, just like human nature itself, which is also imperfect, unlike eternal life after death, considered the real life because of its perfection (Sweeney, 2007; Zamzami et al., 2021). This reinforces the Quranic idea of supreme happiness in eternal life. According to Al-Farabi, earthly life is only a preparatory stage or transition to the afterlife, which can only be achieved through the transformation of the soul. This transformation would take place through the three stages: *nafs al ammarah*, the alert and commanding soul, linked to animal desires and impulses and considered the lowest level of the self; *nafs al lawwamah*, the critical and repentant soul; and *nafs al mutmainnah*, the satisfied and peaceful soul. The struggle against the lower self is a struggle of the soul (*jihad al-nafs*) in search of its evolution in order to lead it to another way of life, where the material world takes on a smaller dimension than the spiritual. This would actually be the purpose of life, which is to enable the subject to achieve eternal happiness after death by overcoming the soul's internal struggle during worldly life.

Al-Farabi points out that religion is natural to man, and so to discard it would be tantamount to eliminating human nature itself (Sweeney, 2007). This is why he argues that being happy is not an easy task and is only possible for those who possess wisdom and a spiritual level high enough to strive for their goals and face difficulties. He argues that only the heart (*qalb*) has the power to control the mind and reveals that the heart stands out as the most important organ in the body, followed by the brain, liver, and others, until reaching the genitals, which would be the least important. According to Al-Farabi, it is the heart that governs and reacts to the stimuli captured by the sense organs. As well as encompassing rational faculties, the heart is also the center of individuals' biological and perceptive abilities (López-Farjeat, 2020). He emphasizes, however, that there must be harmony between the heart and the mind first, so that there is a positive impact on the body's other organs (Iskakuly et al., 2021).

Al-Farabi argues that happiness is everything that is good and desirable, and the most perfect goal that humans have sought since the beginning of their existence. He describes it as a good that is acquired and not something innate, being obtained through divine sanction, detachment from matter, and closeness to God. According to him, there are basically two types of happiness: true happiness, which is desirable for its own sake and not for the sake of other interests, and false happiness, which is focused on pleasure, obtaining material goods, status, and so on. According to him, the greatest happiness is that which is connected to God because all others are doubtful (Zamzami et al., 2021).

For Al-Farabi, perfect happiness cannot be achieved without people's help and without knowing the purpose of human existence. The philosopher argues that human beings first need to know what happiness really is in order to transform it into a purpose and discover how to achieve it. For this to happen, two main elements are needed: knowledge and the practice of virtues, since both represent fixed and stable universal truths that will never change. Thus, as it is something rational, happiness requires the intellect, and in order for the individual to reach the highest level, they need to identify and acquire more knowledge about their talents to put them into practice. Ideally, they should seek knowledge about themselves and all of creation so that this sharpens their perception of the divine magnitude and thus brings them closer to God (Zamzami et al., 2021).

Ibn Miskawayh was also one of the philosophers who developed studies on the subject of happiness. His writings deal with ethics, morals, good manners, and other attitudes that would help individuals achieve happiness. He sees happiness as a process of moral and spiritual purification, in which the individual prepares himself throughout life in order to perfect himself ethically and morally. The lack of these elements is the main cause of human unhappiness. He adds that both physical health and ethical health are necessary to achieve balance. He also stresses the importance of emotional regulation as a way of dealing emotionally with one's mistakes. This moral balance is a constant challenge. For this reason, he suggests that one of the ways to reverse human failings is to exchange bad actions for virtuous ones, just as prescribed in the Quran (Awaad et al., 2021).

In *Tahdhib al-Aklaq*, Ibn Misakwayh emphasizes the importance of refining one's character through ethical precepts, but also through knowledge of these precepts, as they contribute to achieving moral happiness. According to him, there are internal and external conditions for achieving this happiness. The internal conditions are those linked to one's own body, good health, and a moderate temperament, while the external conditions are those present in the subject's environment and necessary for their adaptation, such as goods and the social context. It is in this social context that, according to him, it is possible for the subject to create emotional bonds and practice virtues such as courage, honesty, and generosity, and thus achieve happiness (Al-Din, 1994).

Influenced by Plato's theory of the tripartite soul, Ibn Miskawayh also divides it into reason, spirit, and desires. Desires, according to him, are the soul's lowest level, and the virtue of patience is its greatest antidote, helping the subject resist pleasures, especially those that cause him shame. In the philosopher's view, these pleasures are ways of escaping from pain and immediate needs. He criticizes hedonic pleasures of the body, describing them as false and accidental, and pleasures of the intellect as true and essential. For this reason, the refinement of character is the way to achieve the highest, most complete, and permanent level of happiness—divine happiness (Adamson, 2015). Ibn Miskawayh also mentions the psychological conditions for achieving happiness, which are conditioned by training, purification, and discipline of the soul, as well as awareness of one's own defects. The search for this evolution takes place both through human effort and divine will. This is the way to cure and treat diseases of the soul such as cowardice, pride, arrogance, fear, impulsiveness, ostentation, betrayal, and contempt (Al-Din, 1994).

In their works, various early Muslim scholars argued that virtues were the path to happiness both in this worldly life and in the life after death (Omais et al., 2023). Miskawayh (2003), one of the most prominent names on this topic, argued that to achieve happiness we need to practice virtues systematically and frequently until they become a natural habit, carried out without effort or difficulty. According to this philosopher, the practice of virtues and the development of character would be a type of therapy to restore moral health and preserve the soul's health, thus being a factor as important as caring for the body's health. Both *adab* and *akhlaq*, together with submission and obedience to God, would be essential elements for happiness, as mentioned by the philosopher. As he explains, if a person's evolution occurs from cognition and actions, then knowledge would be the path to perfecting cognition, while morals and character would be the fundamental elements to refine behavior. According to this philosopher, we would achieve happiness through internal conditions such as health, temperament, and attention to one's actions, and external conditions like the ability to overcome one's flaws and weaknesses and to tame one's desires and wishes (Miskawayh, 2003; Rassool, 2021).

Known as the Prince of Physicians, Ibn Sina also played an important role in the study of happiness, being the most prominent name in Islamic medical science (Awaad et al., 2021). He points out that both positive and negative emotions are temporary, and just as there is no absolute happiness, there is also no absolute sadness. Thus, no one can be totally happy or totally unhappy in this world, since there will always be divine gifts in people's lives, whether material or spiritual, as long as they know how to perceive them. Ibn Sina classifies happiness into three categories: bodily or sensual pleasure, internal pleasure, and intellectual pleasure. Regarding the physical category, he reveals that although true happiness lies in the afterlife, human beings should not despise the gifts that God has given them on the worldly plane, since they are given to human beings to enjoy. This includes physical happiness, which should also be appreciated and not ignored. The second category is the identification and bringing together of the forces of the soul to achieve happiness, where there is often a state of internal conflict between reason and human emotions about what is good or bad. The third category is intellectual pleasure, which, for him, is the most lasting happiness (Zamzamani et al., 2021).

In Ibn Sina's view, happiness is achieved through the soul, with acts of worship, intellect, and knowledge about the world and God being the main references for its evolution. The most sublime and perfect happiness, according to him, can only be achieved when individuals include God in all their daily affairs, following and obeying His commands. Religious contemplation and detachment from distractions are also ways of feeling pleasure (Zakaria, 2012), taking the individual's evolution to the highest level. Human beings' only reference for perfection is God, and if happiness is characterized by perfection, there is no way to obtain it except through a connection with God. Thus, only a connection with what is most perfect in existence would make it possible for humans to perfect themselves and perceive the evil that surrounds them, be it internal or external.

Al-Ghazālī, one of the best-known scholars in the Islamic world, especially for his studies of the soul and psyche, reveals a more complete and comprehensive conception of happiness that includes four dimensions: goods of the soul, bodily goods, external goods, and goods of divine grace. The goods of the soul would be formed by faith, which is also synonymous with knowledge and includes religious knowledge and its practice, and by good character, which includes virtues (Al-Ghazali, 1995). Virtues such as justice and temperance favor the practice of other virtues because they are behaviors that repress anger and desires. Bodily goods, according to Al-Ghazali, are also indispensable to happiness and include health, physical strength, longevity, and beauty. External goods, such as wealth, status, and being born into a family that cultivates knowledge and piety, are elements that make an individual's life easier and less painful. On the other hand, goods of divine grace, such as direction, guidance, leadership, and strengthening the connection with the divine, help unite external aspects with aspects of the soul (Sabjan, 2019).

For Al-Ghazālī, there are two mechanisms that distinguish humans from animals and are fundamental for achieving happiness: knowledge and action. The strengthening of knowledge, for him, strengthens the love for God and human spirituality, leading him to right action. He thus unites the internal and external dimensions, emphasizing that tranquility and happiness would only be achieved as long as external human actions were aligned with divine guidelines and prescriptions (Sabjan, 2019). Love of God, according to Al-Ghazali, would be the highest level of happiness and the highest purpose of knowledge, but only those who possess deep divine knowledge could achieve this feeling. Signs of love for God include sincerity and surrender, acceptance of death, constant and spontaneous remembrance of God, and devotion, as well as love for the Quran and the Prophet Muhammad (ﷺ). Death is considered by Al-Ghazali to be the first test of an individual's love of God. According to him, the thought of death would not be a discomfort to those who are prepared to receive it because it is an opportunity for the soul to meet God and also due to actions carried out throughout life (Al-Ghazali, 2001).

Al-Ghazali described a personality structured on the metaphysical representation of four elements mentioned in the Quran: the spirit (*rūḥ*), which would represent the life force and connection with the divine; the ego or soul (*nafs*), representing behavior and its inclinations toward good or evil; the intellect or reason (*aql*), representing cognition and rationality; and the heart (*qalb*), which can be affected positively or negatively depending on the interaction between the other structures (Al-Ghazali, 1995). The concept of the soul in Islam is not separate from the concept of the psyche, since the very translation of the term "psychology" (*ilm an nafs*) from the Arabic language "study of the soul" is similar to the etymology of the word in the Greek language.

Al-Ghazali developed concepts of spiritual diseases of the heart, such as arrogance, greed, ignorance, envy, and lust. In order for individuals to learn to curb these behaviors, they would need to purify their souls (*tazkiyat al-nafs*). He argues that if animals can be trained and domesticated for certain behaviors, it is also possible for humans to modify and perfect their behaviors by training the soul for the purification of the individual. Many of Al-Ghazali's concepts, even before traditional psychological theories, were built on the premise that individuals are constantly evolving and, therefore, their soul or psyche goes through three stages. In the first, according to the Quran (12:53), it inclines toward evil and the most primitive impulses (*nafs al 'ammārah*); in the second, the stage of self-criticism (*nafs al lawwāma*), self-awareness, connection with God, and spirituality help subjects understand and control their instincts and desires; and in the third, when the soul is at peace (*nafs al mutma'innah*). In this last stage, a high level of satisfaction and contentment would be achieved through submission to divine teachings and the individual's union with God (Al-Ghazali, 1995; Keshavarzi & Ali, 2021; Rothman, 2022).

Another prominent philosopher was Ibn Rushd (Averroes), a polymath who emphasized philosophy's position as the highest level of science and happiness, second only to the divine sciences. For Ibn Rushd, there was no difference between philosophy's and religion's aims, since both sought truth and happiness (Awaad et al., 2021). In his view, happiness would be achieved by religious and intellectual virtues together, and not by one to the detriment of the other. He argues that, compared to other, more fleeting pleasures, intellectual happiness is more lasting, hence the need for a harmonious union between reason and faith, arguing that if divine revelation itself invites individuals to reflect on its teachings, then effort and intellectual reasoning would be obligatory for them (Costa, 1994).

Ibn Rushd's hallmark is precisely his attempt to unite philosophy, whose focus is on reason, with the religious teachings of the *Shariah*, which contain moral, ethical, and spiritual concepts that can contribute to the subject's process of happiness. In his work, he connects intellectual, social, and religious virtues with happiness, arguing that rational contemplation and the search for truth alone would be a source of pleasurable sensation (Leaman, 1980).

3.2   Islamic Philosophy and the Revival of Islamic Psychology

It is clear that Islamic philosophy has established itself as a millenary science and a pioneer with various discoveries related to the human psyche. However, the theoretical framework built up by Muslim scholars over the centuries has been rendered invisible by science. Modern psychology is presented in academic environments as a recent science constructed exclusively by exponents of the Western world, completely obscuring other peoples' contributions to current knowledge. Furthermore, the body of work on psychology written by thinkers from the Arab world and Islamic countries has not always received due prominence in the face of the hegemony of Western theories and the coloniality of science. Several works have been lost over time due to the many wars and conflicts in the region, the lack of proper preservation, or even the lack of translation and re-editing of their contents into other languages.

Many contemporary researchers in the field have drawn upon the considerable historical legacy of early Muslim philosophers, physicians, theologians, and scholars to also integrate this epistemological perspective's theoretical repertoire and continue the development of concepts and theoretical models. The ideas and structure originally studied by Philosophy played a central role in Islamic knowledge and ended up serving as the basis for the construction and development of various recent theories in the field of Islamic Psychology. Elements such as the soul (*nafs*), the spirit (*rūḥ*), the intellect (*aql*), and the heart (*qalb*) are present in many passages of the Quran and have been used by many early thinkers and current researchers as a basis for explaining psychic functioning from a systemic interaction in which individuals seek to evolve and improve their attitudes and behaviors continuously throughout life (Keshavarzi & Ali, 2021; Rassool, 2021; Rothman, 2022).

The Islamic legacy ranges from the contributions of early Islamic thinkers to more contemporary ones, showing how important it is to comprehend these philosophical ideas, since many of them are also related to the Islamic conception of well-being. The absence of approaches in the West that included specific peoples' spiritual dimensions and ethnic-cultural and religious particularities has contributed to the emergence of new perspectives that can change the scientific scenario. The revival of Islamic psychology in contemporary times has gained more strength with Professor Malik Badri's works due to his persistence and boldness in defending this paradigm at a time when psychological science was rejecting the inclusion of religion in its theories (Badri, 2016).

Thus, the enrichment of science requires more precise data and information, and epistemological foundations on this subject, based on a multidisciplinary profile, are needed to allow for future experimental research, which is one of the premises of Islamic psychology. Furthermore, the sources of psychosocial suffering that affect the Muslim population are numerous, which also raises the need for studies related to well-being and mental health, linking it to the spiritual resources offered by Islamic teachings.

References

Adamson, P. (2015). Miskawayh on pleasure. *Arabic Sciences and Philosophy, 25*(2), 199–223. https://doi.org/10.1017/s0957423915000028

Al-Din, N. G. (1994). Miskawayh. *Prospects, 24*(1–2), 131–152. https://link.springer.com/content/pdf/10.1007/BF02199012.pdf

Al-Ghazali, A. H. (1995). *Al-Ghazali on disciplining the soul: Kitab Riyadat Al-Nafs & On breaking the two desires. Kitab Kasr Al-Shahwatayn, Books XXII and XXIII of the revival of the religious sciences: Ihya Ulum Al-Din* (T. J. Winter, Trans.). Islamic Texts Society.

Al-Ghazali. (2001). *A Alquimia da Felicidade.* (C. Field Trad.). Fissus.

Attie Filho, M. (2002). *Falsafa: A Filosofia Entre os Árabes.* Palas Athena.

Awaad, R., Elsayed, D., Ali, S., & Abid, A. (2021). Islamic psychology: A portrait of its historical origins and contributions. In H. Keshavarzi, F. Khan, B. Ali, & R. Awaad (Eds.), *Introducing Traditional Islamically Integrated Psychotherapy*, 69–95. Routledge.

Badri, M. (2013). *Abu Zayd Al-Balkhi's Sustenance of the Soul.* The International Institute of Islamic Thought.

Badri, M. (2016). *The dilemma of muslim psychologists.* Islamic Book Trust.

Bukhârî and Muslim. (n.d.). Riyad as-Salihin 224.In-book reference: Introduction, Hadith 224. Sunnah.com. https://sunnah.com/riyadussalihin:224

Costa, J.S. (1994). *Averróis: O Aristotelismo Radical.* .

Iskakuly, D., Kopbossynov, M., Yerkinbayev, U., Alpysbayeva, S., & Kenzhalin, K. (2021). The phenomenon of a happy person in the works of Al-Farabi as a classic expression of poetic images. *International Journal of Society, Culture & Language, 9*(2), 54–63. https://www.ijscl.com/article_244356.html

Keshavarzi, H., & Ali, B. (2021). Foundations of traditional Islamically integrated psychotherapy (TIIP). In H. Keshavarzi, F. Khan, B. Ali, & R. Awaad (Eds.), *Introducing traditional Islamically integrated psychotherapy* (pp. 13–37). Routledge.

Leaman, O. (1980). Ibn Rushd on happiness and philosophy. *Studia Islamica, 52*, 167–181. https://doi.org/10.2307/1595366

López-Farjeat, L. X. (2020). Al-Farabi's psychology and epistemology. In E. N. Zalta (Ed.), *The Stanford encyclopedia of philosophy* (Summer 2020 Edition). https://plato.stanford.edu/archives/sum2020/entries/al-farabi-psych/

Miskawayh, A. (2003). *The Refinement of Character (Tadhib al-Akhlaq)* (S. H. Nasr Trad). Kazi Publications.

Omais, S., Tarif, E., & Santos, M. A. (2023). Ethics, morals, virtues and character strengths: A comparison between Islamic psychology and positive psychology. In C. Y. Al-Karam (Ed.), *The way of love* (pp. 129–152). Al Karam Press.

Rassool, H. (2021). *Islamic psychology: Human behaviour and experience from an Islamic perspective.* Routledge.

Raudah, S. F., Arief, Y., & Rahman, A. A. (2023). Abu Zayd Al-Balkhi's perspective on depression and anxiety in 'Masalih Al-Abdan Wa Al-Anfus'. *Psikis: Jurnal Psikologi Islami, 9*(2), 302–311. https://doi.org/10.19109/psikis.v9i2.19621

Rothman, A. (2022). *Developing a model of Islamic psychology and psychotherapy: Islamic theology and contemporary understandings of psychology.* Routledge.

Sabjan, M. A. (2019). The meaning and experience of happiness in Islam: An overview. *The European Proceedings of Social and Behavioural Sciences.* 10.15405/epsbs.2019.09.44

Sweeney, M. J. (2007). Philosophy and "Jihād:" Al-Fārābī on Compulsion to Happiness. *The Review of Metaphysics, 60*(3), 543–572.

The Clear Quran. (n.d.). (M. Khattab, Trans.). https://Quran.com/

Zakaria, I. (2012). Ibn Sina on 'Pleasure and Happiness'. *Advances in Natural and Applied Sciences, 6*(8), 1283–1286. https://www.aensiweb.com/old/anas/2012/1283-1286.pdf

Zamzami, M., Hosseini, E. A., Gholizadeh, H., Shariati, M. M., Muktafi, M., & A'la, A. (2021). Physical and spiritual dimensions of happiness in the thought of Al-Fārābī and Ibn Sīnā. *Teosofia: Indonesian Journal of Islamic Mysticism, 10*(2), 229–248. https://doi.org/10.21580/tos.v10i2.8629

Chapter 4
Happiness in the Quran

The Quran's authority is unquestionable among Muslims, notwithstanding the different sects. It is also the main guideline for a good and agreeable life (Joshanloo, 2013; Joshanloo & Weijers, 2019). The Quran and *Sunnah* are abundant sources of information about the soul, self-development, and self-knowledge (Munsoor, 2021). Because it is a divine message, the Quran is the principal source for interpreting happiness in Islam, while the *Sunnah* (a collection of sayings and prophetic traditions) codifies it in detail (Al-Attas, 1995). In addition, it is also essential to explore the knowledge left by the classical names in Islamic literature who studied and developed the subject long before it became an object of study in contemporary psychology (Iskandar, 2012; Wahab, 2022).

Sa'adah is the translation of the word happiness in Arabic, and its opposite, unhappiness, is *shaqwah*, which can also be understood as everything linked to suffering, misfortune, and degradation (Nasr, 2014; Sabjan, 2019). The term happiness is translated into Arabic as *sa'adah*, but we can find terms in the Quran with similar meanings, such as *farah* (to rejoice/enjoy), *sakina* (tranquility), *falah* (successful/blessed), *ridha* (contentment), *sa'id* (happy/fortunate), *hasana* (good/virtuous), *naja* (salvation), *mardiyattan* (satisfied), *hayatan ṭayyibatan (pleasant life)*, and *radiyyatan* (satisfied/pleased). In Islam, there is no explicit distinction between happiness and well-being, as can be seen in secular literature. When referring to life after death, the Quran uses more intense terms, such as happiness and rejoicing, while references to worldly life are represented by more restrained and gentler terms, such as contentment, tranquility, or a good life.

The Quran prioritizes happiness related to more permanent and lasting elements rather than that which is temporary and fleeting. It focuses on the human's inner essence, a structure that does not dissipate after death. For Nasr (2014), this is what differentiates the Islamic perspective from one centered on hedonic references. According to the author, the Islamic conception also differs from the Western conception by the very term used in Arabic. Instead of the famous English phrase "pursuit of happiness," Arabic uses the expression *tahssil al-saadah*, translated as the attainment of happiness. Although the difference seems subtle, the latter translation denotes that happiness is in a person's possession, and not something external that he or she needs to achieve.

Although the word "happiness" is present in the Quran through analogous expressions such as contentment, joy, fun, pleasure, and rejoicing, among others, the word *sa'adah* in its literal form is found in only two verses, in contexts associating this emotional state only with those who reach Paradise (Nasr, 2014). The prerequisite for achieving this goal is the alignment of human actions with divine satisfaction. According to Saritoprak and Abu Raiya (2023, p. 182), this is basically the Islamic concept of well-being. They state that "an Islamic understanding of health and well-being holds that a good life is achieved primarily through a life in accordance with Islamic teachings." Although generic, this is perhaps the most succinct and objective way of defining what is considered well-being in Islam, but we need to delve more deeply into religious content to understand the logic buttressing this paradigm.

In general, elements linked to happiness can be internal or external, material or spiritual. Various authors agree that descriptions of happiness in the Quran revolve around a worldly vision and another in the afterlife (Joshanloo, 2013, 2017; Nasr, 2014; Omais & Santos, 2022; Wiliasih et al., 2024). While earthly life is associated with more temporary happiness, eternal life is symbolized by real and lasting contentment as a reward for obedience to divine orders and the efforts employed throughout life (Omais & Santos, 2022; Nasr, 2014; Sabjan, 2019). The happiness described in the Quran is basically divided into two categories. The first would be in relation to time and space, that is, worldly happiness (*dunya*) and eternal happiness in the afterlife (*akhirah*). The second category would be with regard to its characteristics on the earthly plane, that is, real happiness, linked to faith and good deeds, and illusory happiness, which is temporary and connected to wealth and material goods (Fig. 4.1).

In Sabjan's (2019) view, many Western concepts of happiness are shrouded in doubt and uncertainty, just as they were in philosophy, because they limit themselves only to worldly aspects, since many philosophers did not believe in a life

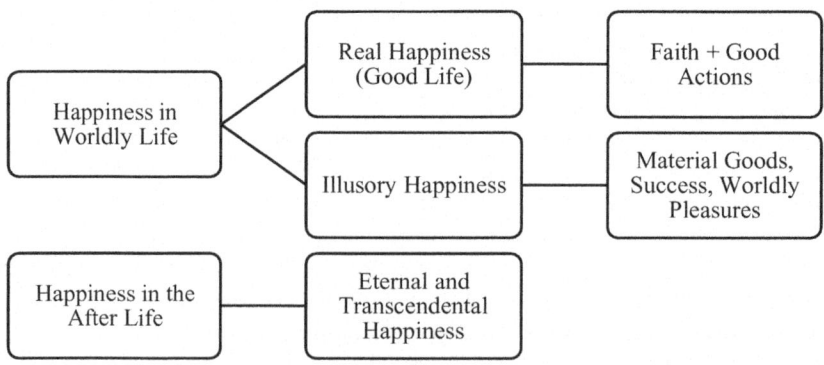

Fig. 4.1 The Quranic vision of happiness—Adapted by the author

beyond the earthly perspective. He reinforces that, although knowledge about death is limited due to the uncertain and nebulous nature permeating the end of human life, many end up exploring the concept of happiness only within the limited spectrum of life. They base their view on the argument that, using traditional science, we can only measure and prove what is present in this dimension. This, however, can make the concept fragile and limited, especially in spiritual and religious aspects.

However, we must stress that this more spiritualized conception of happiness in Islam is not restricted only to the future prospect of another life but also to the present moment. The Quran focuses on both the present and the future simultaneously, through narratives that focus on these two temporal dimensions (Nasr, 2014). For this reason, we can find verses that focus exclusively on the life to come, as well as verses that teach Muslims to beseech divine "gifts" together in both this worldly life and the life to come, as in the passage that says, "Yet there are others who say, 'Our Lord! Grant us the good of this world and the Hereafter, and protect us from the torment of the Fire'" (Quran, 2:201, interpretation of the meaning).

4.1 Happiness in Worldly Life

One of Islamic doctrine's main focuses is to warn human beings that happiness is a short and fleeting experience in its worldly dimension. Although pleasing, it can often be followed by feelings of sadness and dissatisfaction. Perhaps this is why the Quran does not emphasize happiness in worldly life, since there would be no point in building or pursuing something momentary and fleeting, with an end date, restricted only to the present (Nasr, 2014). In Islam, worldly happiness is not an end in itself. It should not be restricted to momentary feelings and emotions. Although eternal happiness is given greater prominence in the Quran, Al-Attas (1995) points out that worldly happiness can be experienced in a lasting way when accompanied by spirituality. Corroborating the Aristotelian view of hedonism and eudaimonism, in the Islamic perspective, worldly happiness is characterized by momentary emotional oscillations, while lasting happiness, which is less frequent, is the result of a virtuous and spiritual life (Al-Attas, 1995).

4.1.1 Illusory Worldly (Hedonic) Happiness

The brevity and temporary nature of human existence correspond, in due proportion, to the temporary nature of hedonic happiness. In the Quran, worldly life is described in two different ways: one as the happiness of pleasures, and the other as spiritual happiness. In the first way, worldly pleasures are portrayed in the Quran as illusory, through terms such as amusement, play, enjoyment, and illusion, as in the verse that says:

> The enjoyment of 'worldly' desires—women, children, treasures of gold and silver, fine horses, cattle, and fertile land—has been made appealing to people. These are the pleasures of this worldly life, but with Allah is the finest destination (Quran, 3:14, interpretation of the meaning).
>
> Know that this worldly life is no more than play, amusement, luxury, mutual boasting, and competition in wealth and children. This is like rain that causes plants to grow, to the delight of the planters. But later the plants dry up and you see them wither, then they are reduced to chaff. And in the Hereafter there will be either severe punishment or forgiveness and pleasure of Allah, whereas the life of this world is no more than the delusion of enjoyment (Quran, 57:20, interpretation of the meaning).

In comparison with eternal life, the description of worldly happiness in the Quran shows that it is generally marked by hedonism, by temporary and fleeting pleasures. The verses cited above exemplify these pleasures as goods, wealth, children, women, lust, property, animals, gambling, as well as behaviors such as rivalry, competitiveness, ostentation, and coveting goods and people. The metaphor of the crop, which, when brought to life and multiplied by rain, gives the growers a momentary joy that soon fades with the passage of time, becoming nothing more than straw, is a comparison that reflects both the temporary nature of worldly happiness and the brevity of the cycle of life.

These metaphors about worldly life's ephemeral nature are portrayed in various verses, reminding Muslims of human existence's fragility and transience, and that even moments of success cannot be permanent. Doctrine gives this warning regarding the illusion of worldly happiness when it exhorts Muslims not to make such earthly achievements their main purpose in life:

> The life of this world is just like rain We send down from the sky, producing a mixture of plants which humans and animals consume. Then just as the earth looks its best, perfectly beautified, and its people think they have full control over it, there comes to it Our command by night or by day, so We mow it down as if it never flourished yesterday! This is how We make the signs clear for people who reflect (Quran, 10:24, interpretation of the meaning).

A question then arises: if the Quran portrays worldly life as an ephemeral and illusory pleasure, and if the only verses in the Quran that mention the term happiness (*sa'adah*) refer to life after death, then does Islam not believe in the existence of happiness on the earthly plane? Yes, it does exist, but it is momentary and incomparable to eternal life. The Quran emphasizes that Muslims should not allow themselves to be seduced by the pleasures of life that give them peaks of happiness and should not create expectations or make this their purpose in life. The Quran explains: "This worldly life is no more than play and amusement. But the Hereafter is indeed the real life, if only they knew!" (Quran, 29:64, interpretation of the meaning). This passage confirms that it is eternal life Muslims long for. However, because it is a distant reality, it often ends up being neglected for the present moment.

When translated literally, the word *dunya*, representing worldly life in the Arabic language, means underworld or lower life (Munsoor, 2021). It represents life's temporary and fleeting nature, distracting individuals from their future goal, the life that will follow, eternal life. Hedonic happiness in worldly life is not condemned in the Quran, but it is presented as a significantly lesser, superficial, and fleeting form of contentment than eternal happiness. Worldly happiness is understood as only a sample of what Muslims consider true happiness: eternal happiness after death (Wahab, 2022). However, this does not mean that individuals should renounce life and live only waiting for death. There would be no point in that, and if that were the case, many might even take their own lives to speed up the process. However, the Quran advises Muslims not to comit suicide, not to despair of divine mercy (Quran, 4:29) and not to allow themselves to be carried away by despair and hopelessness. Thus, worldly life must be lived actively, with a constant reminder of death but without passively awaiting its arrival. The remembrance of death and the Last Judgement is the motivating element that encourages individuals to remain vigilant and monitor their behavior in order to be accountable before God.

At the same time, Islam teaches that the good and lawful things obtained during earthly life should be enjoyed, as they are God's gifts to humans. Muslims should not reject or refrain from enjoying the lawful pleasures that God has given them in life in the name of asceticism. There are verses in the Quran that mention that God has reserved a reward for Muslims in both this life and the Hereafter, warning that they should enjoy what God has given them as a form of gratitude, even though no earthly pleasure is comparable to those of the Hereafter: "[...] For those who do good in this world, there is goodness. But far better is the ʿeternalʾ Home of the Hereafter. How excellent indeed is the home of the righteous" (Quran, 16:30, interpretation of the meaning). Another verse states:

> Rather, seek the ʿrewardʾ of the Hereafter by means of what Allah has granted you, without forgetting your share of this world. And be good ʿto othersʾ as Allah has been good to you. Do not seek to spread corruption in the land, for Allah certainly does not like the corruptors (Quran, 28:77, interpretation of the meaning).

This verse makes it clear that one should not renounce the world and forget oneself in order to live only for eternal life. There must be a balance, which both the Quran and the *Sunnah* emphasize. It is important to clarify this idea to dispel any association with a life of seclusion, renunciation, or asceticism. If this were the case, the Islamic religion would not consider ordinary acts of daily life as acts of worship but would restrict worship to only certain rituals, as seen in this passage from the Quran that broadly defines virtue:

> Righteousness is not in turning your faces towards the east or the west. Rather, the righteous are those who believe in Allah, the Last Day, the angels, the Books, and the prophets; who give charity out of their cherished wealth to relatives, orphans, the poor, ʿneedyʾ travellers, beggars, and for freeing captives; who establish prayer, pay alms-tax, and keep the pledges they make; and who are patient in times of suffering, adversity, and in ʿthe heat ofʾ battle. It is they who are true ʿin faithʾ, and it is they who are mindful ʿof Allahʾ (Quran, 2:177, interpretation of the meaning).

According to Ibn Kathir (Quran.com, n.d.), the piety and righteousness (*al-birr*) described in this verse have a broad meaning, which, in addition to belief in the pillars of faith and the performance of rituals, also urges obedience, righteous behavior, and the practical implementation of divine commands in both individual and social spheres. This verse is also important for guiding those individuals who isolate themselves or renounce life in order to devote themselves exclusively to religion, due to misinterpretations about the real concept of spirituality from an Islamic point of view.

4.1.2 Real Worldly (Eudaimonic) Happiness and the "Pleasant Life"

So what would eudaimonic happiness, or a good life, look like in Islam? Positive psychology has only existed for a little more than two decades, while the teachings of the Quran, an ancient book that is more than 1400 years old, already mention the term "good life." According to the Quranic verse, "Whoever does good, whether male or female, and is a believer, We will surely bless them with a good life, and We will surely reward them according to the best of their deeds." (Quran, 16:97, interpretation of the meaning).

The term "good life" is somewhat similar to Aristotle's (2003) concept of the good life and eudaimonism, although the philosophical concept does not include religious belief as an essential element for happiness, unlike the Islamic view, which establishes faith as the main basis for a good and virtuous life. We can also say that the relationship between faith and good deeds is reciprocal, each feeding the other. From an Islamic perspective, spirituality is strengthened as it is put into practice in the form of actions. In the same way, good deeds also need a solid belief in the pillars of faith, because it is this belief (*Iman*) that acts as an intrinsic motivating element, creating meaning and giving deeper significance to human actions. A simplified illustration of this concept of well-being can be seen in Fig. 4.2.

While complex, the Quran also manages to convey clarity and simplicity in its teachings, emphasizing that human happiness is found in basic elements that are within everyone's reach and cultivated from the inside out. If we observe the configuration of the verses of the Quran, the sequence of words and admonitions, we can see that faith and good deeds are present in the vast majority of them, making the interdependence between them perceptible. Although spirituality is expected to play a central role, since this approach to well-being is directly associated with a religious perspective, the Quranic vision clearly explains the holistic and integrative paradigm of Islam, which unites human and spiritual acts in a single dimension.

Another point that deserves to be highlighted concerns ethics, morals, and behavior (*akhlaq* and *adab*). When mentioning virtuous attitudes and conduct, the verses

Fig. 4.2 The reciprocal dynamic between faith/ beliefs and good deeds (Quran, 16:97)—Adapted by the author

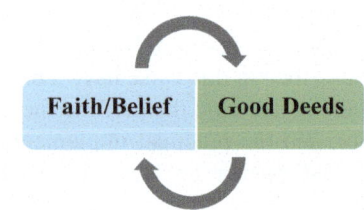

of the Quran usually end by citing God and some of His attributes, the so-called 99 names of God or *asmaa el husna*. In addition to divine qualities, many of these attributes are also related to virtues and ethical and moral behavior. God adds His own qualities in these verses as a way of inspiring humans, even though the creature is far from reaching levels as high as the Creator. This is visible, for example, in passages of the Quran that encourage the practice of forgiveness among human beings, citing Allah's Mercy at the end of the verse, as in the following passage: "Let them pardon and forgive. Do you not love to be forgiven by Allah? And Allah is All-Forgiving, Most Merciful" (24:22). Another example concerns love, mentioned in the verse: "As for those who believe and do good, the Most Compassionate will 'certainly' bless them with 'genuine' love" (19:96), and also generosity: "The example of those who spend their wealth in the cause of Allah is that of a grain that sprouts into seven ears, each bearing one hundred grains. And Allah multiplies 'the reward even more' to whoever He wills. For Allah is All-Bountiful, All-Knowing" (2:261). When encouraging the pursuit of knowledge and reflection, many verses end by mentioning the Omniscience and Wisdom of Allah, as in the verse: "Be mindful of Allah, for Allah 'is the One Who' teaches you. And Allah has 'perfect' knowledge of all things" (2:282). Quranic content that encourages justice and fair and equal treatment among human beings also ends its verses by connecting this virtue with divine attributes, as quoted in the verse: "But if you judge between them, then do so with justice. Surely Allah loves those who are just" (5:42). It can be seen that this connection between divine attributes and the encouragement of virtuous behavior is further proof that faith, that is, the spiritual aspect, and good deeds, which refer to *adab* and *akhlaq*, go hand in hand in Islam, being the fundamental ingredients for a pleasant life.

Islam points to the possibility of achieving a more significant and lasting happiness than hedonic happiness in worldly life, although it can never reach the same magnitude as the transcendental and eternal happiness of the afterlife. It can also be seen from the verse quoted that, according to the Quran, the recipe for this good life is based on two main foundations: faith and good deeds. Another Quranic passage also cites this orientation in a similar way, explaining: "Cooperate with one another in goodness and righteousness, and do not cooperate in sin and transgression." (Quran, 5:2, interpretation of the meaning). Although they are mentioned succinctly in the Quran, both belief and good deeds are broad terms that branch out into various elements (Fig. 4.3). Each element represented in this figure will be explained in more detail in the following topics.

4.1.2.1 Faith, Beliefs, and Good Deeds

The lack of a strong belief system built on solid values that give meaning to life leads to doubt, insecurity, and confusion. The concepts relating to happiness and well-being in Islam have a linear characteristic because they present an objective perspective based on the same elements as faith. For this reason, in Islam, faith is considered to be the root of character and the driving force for doing good, bearing

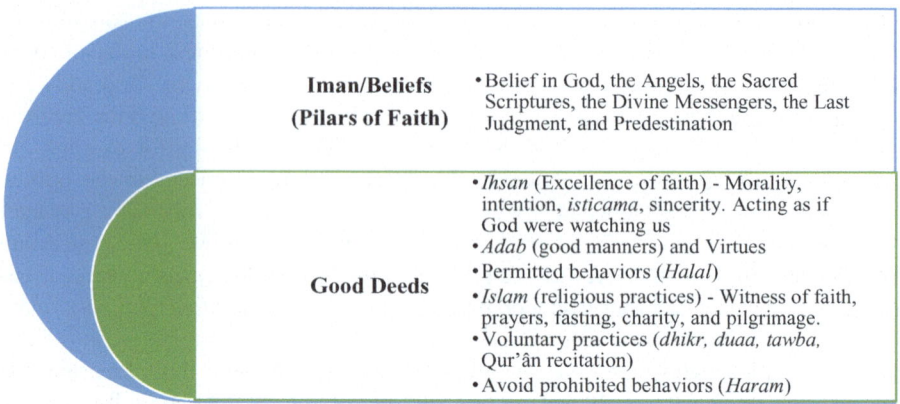

Fig. 4.3 The Quranic model for a pleasant life based on faith and good deeds (Quran, 16:97)—
Adapted by the author

a close relationship with moral conduct (Ihsan et al., 2023). Understanding the
extent of this allows us to understand the driving force directing some Muslims'
behavior and how this intrinsic motivation can mobilize them toward action and
processes of change. The main source of virtue is faith (*Iman*) in God, which is why
the word faith in Quranic verses always precedes the recommendation to do good
deeds. It is the support, the root that nourishes human actions, characterizing religion's metaphysical/transcendental aspect (Tajul Ariffin et al., 2022). Awareness
and remembrance of God bring tranquility to the soul, freeing it from the worry
generated by doubt, fear, and anguish about the future.

Faith (*Iman*) is the basis of everything. It is the deep conviction that begins and
consolidates internally with the acceptance of faith in the heart and is then externalized through actions (Kasule, 2004). Kasule explains that there are 72 levels of
Iman, the highest of which is belief that there is no god but God (Allah), and the
lowest of which is the act of removing an obstacle from one's path. Levels of faith
can also fluctuate, increasing or decreasing according to the good or bad actions that
individuals undertake (Kasule, 2004; Mazloum, 2010). This fluctuation in the levels
of faith will also determine the greater or lesser influence of religion and its precepts
on an individual's behavior. In Islamic doctrine, motivation is centered around faith
(*Iman*). The word *Iman* is mentioned more than 700 times in the Koran and represents the greatest motivating force in Islam, Muslims' main intrinsic motivation. As
well as being the central axis of motivation, it is also individuals' highest level of
knowledge and confidence, and it is this that helps them maintain, monitor, or modify their behavior. Faith in God (*Iman*) is a force that spreads across all individuals'
dimensions, influencing cognitions, emotions, and behavior. It also directs free will
and decision-making (Alawneh, 2022).

Faith (*Iman*) is the great root that sustains the Muslim religion's other elements.
Islam's six pillars are belief in God, angels, holy books and scriptures, all divine
messengers, the Day of Judgment, and predestination (divine decree). All these

beliefs influence behavior and the practice of good deeds. Prophetic stories serve as inspiration and strength for Muslims, playing a very important motivational role, as do the lessons and guidelines found in the holy scriptures, which encourage or discourage certain behaviors. The belief in angels who take note of and observe human actions and the belief in a day of reckoning when everyone will be held accountable for their actions also guide Muslims' conduct and choices. Belief in predestination and divine designs is a resource that helps relieve anxiety and worry, as well as facilitate the process of acceptance in the face of facts over which human beings have no control. As well as being an act of submission and trust in divine wisdom, this belief in *qadr* is of utmost importance because it contributes to the process of resilience. By accepting God's designs, individuals are prevented from blaming themselves or rebelling against God. This helps them exercise patience and curbs their despair and anguish. Said belief also helps individuals re-establish mental, emotional, and spiritual balance and get back on their feet in search of new paths and solutions. This whole set of awareness that makes up faith collaborates in positively or negatively reinforcing human behavior, either through the expectation of reward or the fear of punishment.

Ghauri (2011) explains that without a logical and connected structure of belief, subjects are at the mercy of only their free will, the limited universe of knowledge that human science provides them with, and their ability to self-regulate and motivate themselves. According to Mazloum (2010, p. 39), a strong connection with God gives humans a state where they "do not fear when people fear, do not despair when all despair, do not fail when others fail [...]" because faith becomes their main support, which is reinforced by the Quran (12:87): "And do not lose hope in the mercy of Allah, for no one loses hope in Allah's mercy except those with no faith." Conviction, submission, and unconditional obedience to God, placing oneself as His servant, as well as fidelity to the Prophet Muhammad (ﷺ), are commitments that reinforce the maintenance of behavior and abstention from certain worldly pleasures (Ghauri, 2011).

The Islamic creed (*aaqidah*) is an important basis for understanding in depth the motivations and cognitions that drive Muslims' behavior. Belief (*Iman*) and trust in God (*tawakkul*) are key elements for a Muslim's well-being, as they underpin the other beliefs. Trust in God (*tawakkul*) is a belief that helps the individual replace negative expectations or perceptions with a more optimistic outlook on life's events (Ağılkaya-Şahin, 2024). The tripod formed by trust, hope, and optimism is directly linked to faith, which is why spirituality plays such an important role when it comes to well-being.

For Tajul Ariffin et al. (2022), belief in the pillars of faith not only consolidates *Iman* but also helps individuals have a positive outlook on life and have the patience to endure challenging moments. Confidence helps reduce negative feelings such as fear, insecurity, guilt, frustration, anxiety, sadness, and more. Hope and optimism create better expectations about the future, invigorate energy and the emotional state, and with this, the possibility of a scenario of change can end up serving as an impetus for action. In the field of action and achievement, persistence and perseverance are fundamental ingredients, but in order for them to be sustained, a foundation is needed with strong attributes such as faith, optimism, hope, and optimism. Although it may seem like an abstract emotion, hope motivates individuals spiritually to build their goals around a purpose, propelling them into action. Hope for forgiveness or for divine reward is an important motivator of this process, generating an interlacing of faith, trust, hope, optimism, patience, and perseverance (Fig. 4.4). Without hope, it becomes more difficult to remain patient in order to achieve a certain goal or to persevere for the sake of enduring difficulties. This relationship among hope, patience, and perseverance may be related to common disorders in our society such as anxiety and depression. An anxious person is usually impatient, unable to postpone gratification or withstand waiting. Similarly, depressed people are unlikely to persist in their long-term goals because of the pessimism and hopelessness they carry. So, if the pillar that sustains hope in Islam is trust in God (*tawakkul*), the lack of this element undermines not only hope itself but all the other structures that depend on it, such as patience and perseverance. Trust in God (*tawakkul*) is an antidote to the doubts permeating human life, both those related to not knowing the future as well as the decisions to be made, situations that tend to cause anguish, anxiety, fear, and affliction. The Qur'an enjoins: "Once you make a decision, put your trust in Allah. Surely Allah loves those who trust in Him" (3:159), and also "Whoever puts their trust in Allah, then He 'alone' is sufficient for them" (65:3). It is therefore understood that trust in Allah (*tawakkul*) is a decisive element for Muslims to have the tranquility and courage to act, to stay resolute in their

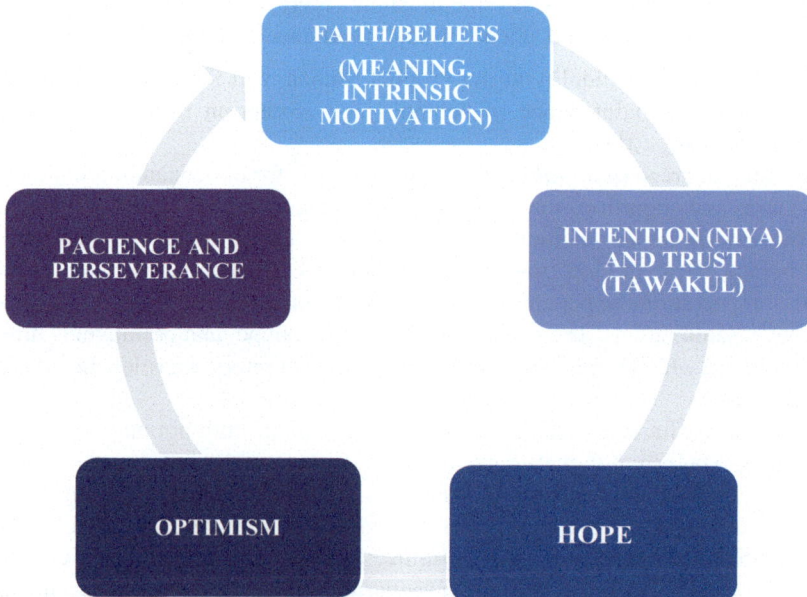

Fig. 4.4 Intrinsic motivation based on faith and beliefs—Elaborated by the author

purpose and objectives without retreating or allowing themselves to be paralyzed by fear and insecurity.

Faith is not merely an abstract or self-sustaining belief. It needs to be nourished in order to grow stronger, through both knowledge and action. For this, two other fundamental elements complement it: *Islam* and *Ihsan*. The concepts of *Islam*, *Iman*, and *Ihsan* originated from a prophetic narration (*Hādīth*), which mentions each of these terms. *Islam* is the externalization of faith and the prerequisite for *Iman*. It acts as an intermediary, connecting the individual with God (Kasule, 2004). Its first step is the testimony of faith (*shahada*) in God and the Prophet Muhammad (ﷺ), followed by obligatory religious practices such as prayers (*salat*), Ramadan fasting (*siyam*), charity (*zakat*), and pilgrimage (*hajj*). The practices of *Islam* can be both forms of worship and ways of developing virtues and noble qualities of character. We can see this, for example, in fasting, a practice that exercises skills and virtues such as self-control, patience, generosity, humility, spirituality, and persistence, among others.

Ihsan, on the other hand, represents the level of excellence of faith, perfection in acts of worship, religious practices, and individuals' conduct in society. It means, according to a Hādīth of the Prophet (ﷺ), "It is that you should serve Allah as though you could see Him, for though you cannot see Him yet (know that) He sees you" (Muslim). Muhsin (2022) states that the term *Ihsan* appears in the Quran 70 times. He explains that awareness of God (*taqwa*) and belief in His presence, observing everything at all times, is a way of creating greater responsibility for individuals. The idea of being watched would be an incentive for them to try their hardest, behave in the best possible way, and do their best to please God. The relationship between this belief and behavior has been studied by researchers under the name of the supernatural monitoring hypothesis. A literature review by Saleam and Moustafa (2016) found that when individuals believe they are being watched by God or other supernatural agents such as angels, there is an increased likelihood that they will behave prosocially.

Ihsan warns individuals that God will know whatever they do, even if no human knows or finds out (Mushin, 2022). It makes Muslims bear in mind that they are under surveillance, and thus they avoid doing things that they would not do if they were not being watched. By understanding the meaning of this phrase, Muslims make decisions more cautiously, being aware that "God is watching" everything they do, and even if they deceive or hide something from people, they cannot hide anything from God. For this reason, *Ihsan* is considered to be the highest of the three elements and, at the same time, the juncture of all of them and everything else that leads to spiritual excellence both in individuals' relationship with God and with people. It is the union of faith (*Iman*) with moral conduct (*akhlaq* and *adab*) and ethics, both in religious rituals and in actions, words, daily conduct, obedience to God and His commandments, and abstention from all that is forbidden. It is through *Ihsan* that good behavior is encouraged, and this can be exemplified in the Quranic verse that teaches that an attitude of kindness toward an enemy can turn him into a close friend: "Good and evil cannot be equal. Respond 'to evil' with what is best, then the one you are in a feud with will be like a close friend" (Quran, 41:34).

The practice of *Ihsan* can influence individuals' well-being. According to Kadhim et al. (2017), *Ihsan* has positive effects both on individuals, in terms of moral and personality development, and on the social environment, strengthening the bonds between people and encouraging behavior that promotes security and harmony in society. The author explains that *Ihsan* has a vertical dimension, which is the excellence of faith with regard to religious rituals and the connection with God, and a horizontal dimension, which refers to Muslims' behavior toward their peers. This shows a relationship of interdependence between God, individuals, and society. Tajul Ariffin et al. (2022) revealed in their research that the practice of *Ihsan* showed positive results on participants' physical and psychological/mental health, and quality of life. The authors explain that *Ihsan* contributes to the development of consciousness and the evolution of individuals from a more instinctive and animal condition to a spiritual condition closer to God. This spiritual evolution, in turn, is externalized through more ethical conduct that can positively influence individuals' mental health. Despite not having defined pillars, there are important elements related to *Ihsan* that also involve behavior, such as obedience, sincerity (*ikhlass*), intention (*niya*), firmness of purpose, righteousness (*isticama*), kindness, and excellence, i.e., striving to do one's best in both conduct and religious practices (Mazloum, 2010). Other characteristics encouraged in addition to purity of intent are modesty, conscientiousness, the pursuit of excellence and quality in all actions, good conduct, and adherence only to what is permitted by religion, avoiding what is doubtful (Tajul Ariffin et al., 2022; Kasule, 2004).

From the Islamic perspective, true freedom comes when individuals live and act in accordance with their original nature, *fitrah*, the pure and good nature that originates with them at birth. Babies and children are closest to this pure nature, but as they grow, depending on their context, they can distance themselves from that original state. It is then through virtue and the practice of good that individuals have the chance to maintain or reconnect with the nature in which they were created. According to Al-Attas (1995), religious virtues are divided into two types: external (*zahir*) and internal. External virtues are those related to religious practices directed only at God, such as the pillars of *Islam* (testimony of faith, prayers, fasting, pilgrimage, charity), remembrance of God (*dhikr*), respect for prohibitions, and the rules of social etiquette. Internal virtues are those linked to the heart, anchored in knowledge and divine revelation. Requirements for these virtues are good intention (*niyah*), actions carried out for a sincere purpose, sincerity, upright conduct, and obedience.

Akhlaq, an Arabic term derived from *khuluq*, translates as disposition, morality, character, customs, or good behavior. Faith is a more abstract and internal concept, while good deeds are the externalization of faith, making it concrete and beneficial to other people. Adherence to ethical and moral norms, when externalized through good deeds, generates benefits not only for society but also for the individual. Both the teachings of the Quran and scientific data prove this. A recent study by Nabi (2024), for example, found a positive relationship between *akhlaq*, life satisfaction, and positive emotions, and a negative relationship with stress and negative emotions. The Quran had already confirmed this result more than 1400 years ago by revealing that "If you act rightly, it is for your own good, but if you do wrong, it is to your own loss" (Quran, 17:7, interpretation of the meaning).

In her work *Quranic Psychology*, Laleh Bakhtiar (2019) states that psychology without ethics does not align with the Islamic vision, since the Quran is a book filled with ethical and moral teachings, the practice of which is essential to achieve health of the soul and well-being on both an individual and social level. One of the verses encouraging the practice of virtues prescribes: "[...] Engage in the practice of good deeds, for wherever you are, God will make you all appear before Him, for God is Almighty" (2:148, interpretation of the meaning). These good deeds are represented by any and all conduct that generates benefit for someone. This includes kindness, ethics, morality, and good manners (*akhlaq* and *adab*), prosocial behavior, and virtues in general (Ishan et al., 2023). Utz (2011) emphasizes that all behavior in line with Shariah and carried out with sincere intentions is considered an act of worship, just like traditional religious rituals.

Islam values acts of kindness regardless of their scale, even if they are simple or trivial. Everything counts as a good deed. Reason and cognition are guided by character and morality (*akhlaq*), giving the soul stability, while *adab* complements *akhlaq* by consolidating and concretizing it through attitude and behavior. Good manners (*adab*), like virtues, are behaviors linked to the divine nature that encourage individuals to remember God daily when practicing them (Al-Kaysi, 2003). This also explains why faith and good deeds appear in combination in the Quran. The goal of good character (*akhlaq*) is happiness in this life and the next. It can be innate or may also be developed through habit and practice, training the intellect to think and reflect in order to achieve wisdom. Unlike animal faculties, which are characterized by impulsiveness and perception, it is humans' rational and cognitive faculties that mobilize and command the body's actions (Al-Attas, 1995). Utz (2011) reinforces that as virtuous behavior becomes a habit, it can even become part of individuals' personality.

Good deeds are related to faith in many ways. One is by influencing the strengthening or weakening of faith. The level of faith (*Iman*) grows according to individuals' actions, which is to say that it is strengthened by obedience to God and His precepts and weakened by disobedience (Utz, 2011). *Akhlaq* is one of the highest forms of faith and occupies such a prominent place in Islam that, in some Hādīths, it is even compared to certain religious acts. An example would be the Hādīth that says, "A believer will attain by his good behaviour the rank of one who prays during the night and observes fasting during the day" (Abū Dāwūd). There is an intrinsic relationship between virtues and spirituality, as such behaviors oppose materialism and are important requirements of faith by externalizing it in the form of actions. Cultivating character goes hand in hand with religious teachings. In Islam, it is also considered a spiritual practice. Thus, while in the Western perspective, spirituality is simply a force of character isolated from others, and the motivation for the person to do good deeds is basically up to free will, in Islam, in addition to the latter, religion also acts as another powerful motivator to encourage good behavior (Fig. 4.5).

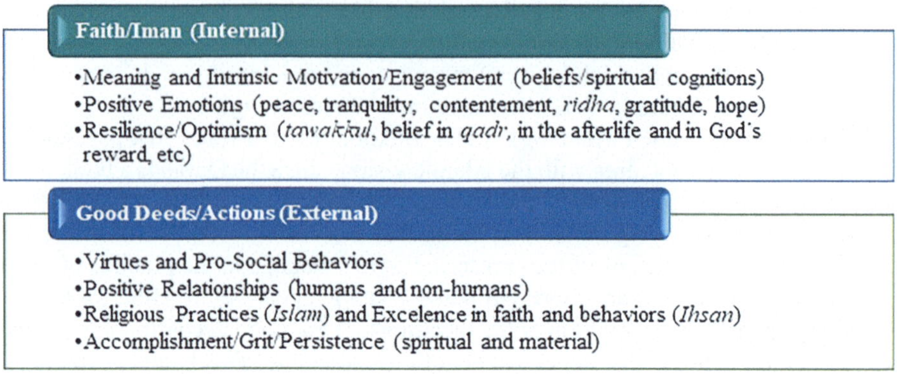

Faith/Iman (Internal)
•Meaning and Intrinsic Motivation/Engagement (beliefs/spiritual cognitions)
•Positive Emotions (peace, tranquility, contentement, *ridha*, gratitude, hope)
•Resilience/Optimism (*tawakkul*, belief in *qadr*, in the afterlife and in God's reward, etc)
Good Deeds/Actions (External)
•Virtues and Pro-Social Behaviors
•Positive Relationships (humans and non-humans)
•Religious Practices (*Islam*) and Excelence in faith and behaviors (*Ihsan*)
•Accomplishment/Grit/Persistence (spiritual and material)

Fig. 4.5 Elements of well-being based on faith and good deeds—Adapted by the Author

Spirituality
Pilars of faith (beliefs)
Fitrah (pure nature)
Sincerity in intentions (*niya*)
Character development and God-Cosciousness (*taqwa*)
Virtues and Good deeds

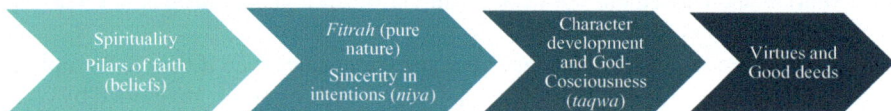

Fig. 4.6 Elements necessary for the practice of virtues in the Islamic view—Adapted by the Author

Personal Traits
Signature Strengths
Meaning-Making and Free Will
Virtues and Character Strengths (individual well-being)

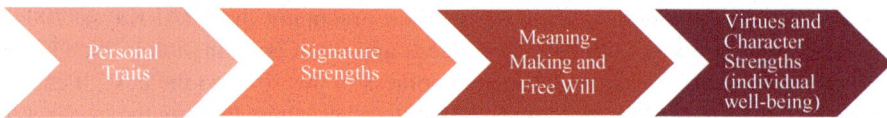

Fig. 4.7 Elements necessary for the practice of virtues in the secular view—Adapted by the Author

Hence, in the Islamic view, for virtuous behavior to become natural and easy to perform does not depend on individuals' will or the presence of certain traits or strengths in their personality (Fig. 4.6). Rather, it depends on their level of spiritual development (Fig. 4.7). The greater the person's connection with God, the greater is their connection with their *fitrah*. This is what will make it easier or not to practice virtues, even in the most challenging circumstances (Omais et al., 2023).

This cycle formed between faith and good deeds is a reciprocal process. Just as the practice of good deeds, reinforced by faith, gives individuals a sense of tranquility and contentment, the absence of these practices will cause them to distance themselves from God and their *fitrah*. This, in turn, may bring them some internal imbalance or disorder, placing them in a state of distress. Such a scenario is portrayed in the Quranic verse: "And by the soul and by Him who formed it, then with the knowledge of right and wrong inspired it! Successful indeed is he who purifies his soul, and damned is he who corrupts it!" (Quran, 91:7–10, interpretation of the meaning).

It is worth emphasizing again that, although beliefs and good deeds are explained separately throughout this book, both are interconnected. The Qur'an itself conceptualizes the term "believer" very broadly, mixing elements related to both faith itself and to good conduct and spiritual practices, as the following verse reveals:

Successful indeed are the believers, those who humble themselves in prayer; those who avoid idle talk; those who pay alms-tax; those who guard their chastity, except with their wives or those 'bondwomen' in their possession, for then they are free from blame, but whoever seeks beyond that are the transgressors; the believers are also' those who are true to their trusts and covenants; and those who are 'properly' observant of their prayers (Quran, 23:1–11)

The practice of good deeds needs to be preceded by knowledge, awareness, and important values that merge with spirituality. Morality, in the Quran's view, embodies monotheism first and foremost, belief in life after death, purity and sincerity of intentions, and, most importantly, piety and awareness of God (*taqwa*). According to Ali (2015), without these elements crystallized in the person, human laws would not be enough to curb people's impulses. Virtues and good deeds appear in very broad forms in both the Qur'an and the *Sunnah*.

We must point out that one of the greatest inspirations for Muslims to practice good deeds is the Prophet Muhammad's (ﷺ) exemplary model of conduct. The Quran itself (68:4) bears witness to this, stating, "because (you) are of the most noble character." The Prophet's (ﷺ) conduct exhibited virtues such as compassion, love, gratitude, generosity, firmness, modesty, fairness, justice, courage, freedom, and a state of contentment and satisfaction, which together serve as inspiration for his followers' behavior (Munsoor, 2021).

4.2 Happiness in the Afterlife

Worldly happiness is incomplete, imperfect, and full of mishaps, with brief, temporary pleasures that constantly need to be repeated and renewed. This repetition over time generates a craving for new, successive, and more intense pleasurable experiences due to hedonic adaptation, a process that can contribute to mental and spiritual illness in the long term. This is why Mazloum (2010) highlights the importance of the Prophet Muhammad's (ﷺ) teaching that Muslims should not become excessively attached to worldly life, according to the Ḥadīth: "Be in this life as if you were a stranger, and act as if you were passing through!" As secular society has loosened its grip on religion and its rules, resisting hedonic pleasures has become an arduous process that depends solely and exclusively on free will, human will, and self-control, even though human laws exist to curb certain behaviors. Consequently, freedom without borders places all the burden of decision-making and the ability to self-regulate the ego's impulses on the human being, making it difficult to delimit hedonic pleasure and the unbridled search for immediate gratification. Evolving spiritually, in this case, becomes a more challenging process since, from a spiritual point of view, by opting for illicit behavior, the person would be more attached to matter and worldly pleasures than to a future reward. It is at this point that internal conflict sets in (Joshanloo & Weijers, 2019).

Spiritual and religious norms and the belief in divine justice exist so that society is not solely at the mercy of individual members of society's goodwill, or of merely human rules, which are often constructed or put into effect only to serve certain groups' interests. Belief in divine judgment and in life after death has a direct influence on human decisions. Every human decision is based on criteria and values assimilated by people. Secularization has eliminated religious rules from this process, leaving human beings at the mercy of only two filters: human laws and their own free will, as illustrated in Fig. 4.8. Although free will can be used in a healthy and coherent way, we cannot say that this is a reality for everyone. Science has proven that the abundance of options surrounding human beings may end up negatively affecting their well-being. For an extended period of time, societies focused on self-determination and overvaluing individual choices have crystallized the idea that this is one of the paths to happiness. However, Roets et al. (2012, p. 700) state that "the high value attached to personal choice is a blessing or a curse may depend on how the individual tends to cope with this (excess of) freedom."

Mustaffa and Akthir (2019) point out that, although we associate the concept of real happiness in Islam with eternal life, attaining it depends on actions in worldly life. Real worldly happiness, in turn, comes from knowledge and good deeds. In this conception of worldly happiness, the authors state that there are factors in common among the traditional philosophical perspective, the Islamic paradigm, and positive psychology. These include encouraging knowledge, the practice of meditation and/or contemplation, the practice of virtues, and the cultivation of social relationships. However, while in the Western view, studies on well-being and happiness are restricted to the earthly plane, in the Islamic view, we cannot explore this subject without considering the happiness expected in the afterlife, since this belief directs and influences cognitions, behaviors, and the very emotions the person experiences.

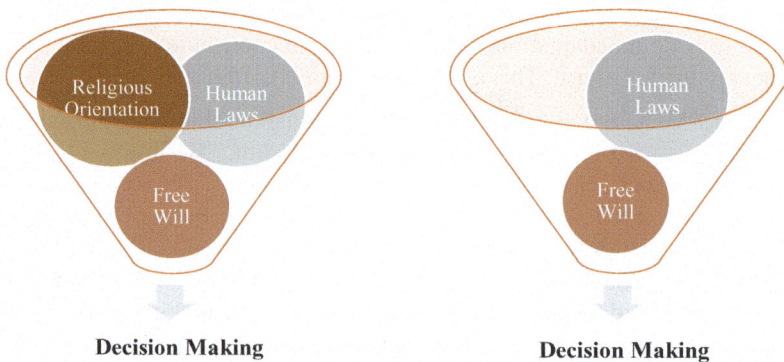

Fig. 4.8 Elements that influence the decision-making process—Adapted by the author

In order to evolve spiritually and follow religious precepts, individuals often need to give up their desires or face deprivations which, at first, may not generate short-term positive emotions such as joy or pleasure. It can, however, generate a state of satisfaction and tranquility due to compliance with religious norms. Such abdication is only possible when there is a purpose that goes beyond the individual sphere, to the point where people exchange their desire or impulse for obedience to God. There is an interesting difference here between the secular and Islamic perspectives on well-being. The secular psychological view rarely encourages individuals to deprive themselves of something, of a desire, except when such abdication is intended to lead them to a future fulfillment limited to the worldly perspective. More often than not, this fulfillment is of a material nature. The Islamic paradigm focuses on material detachment, the postponement of certain gratifications to a more suitable context, and the abdication of certain behaviors for a long-term reality that transcends matter and earthly life. This reality symbolizes a future goal rather than a present one, an eternal purpose rather than a momentary one, and something great unlike anything human beings can imagine. It is a purpose based on belief and faith, but it also has an invisible dimension, since human science cannot measure it. The connection with a purpose, with a greater cause, and with the expectation of real and eternal happiness in the future are factors that encourage individuals to sacrifice some of their desires, putting them in second place. Therefore, if personal desire is no longer the central focus, spiritual well-being becomes a decisive element for subjective well-being.

The relationship between practicing virtues and good deeds and the expectation of a future benefit may be a source of criticism for some people because such behaviors are linked to a future reward and not to the action itself. We must emphasize, however, that although some individuals act virtuously and unpretentiously, which is, in fact, very noble behavior, can we realistically say that all human beings on Earth, from different cultural, educational, social, or economic levels, would be capable of achieving this level of evolution? Several studies have already proven the positive relationship between belief in life after death and mental health and/or well-being. Belief in life after death influences moral decision-making and encourages the adoption of prosocial behaviors (Atkinson & Bourrat, 2011). In addition, it reduces existential doubts in human beings, reduces feelings of distress and anxiety in the face of death, and also gives more meaning to life (Ellison et al., 2009; Flannelly et al., 2006). The expectation of reward in the future increases individuals' tolerance for adversity and suffering, giving them more strength and hope (Al-Issa et al., 2021; Flannelly et al., 2006; Ellison et al., 2009). It further reduces the sense of urgency for immediate pleasures and gratifications and attachment to the material world's pleasures (Ahaddour & Broeckaert, 2018). Belief in divine judgment and its promise of justice generates relief and tranquility for those who suffer injustices throughout life (Ellison et al., 2009), reducing pain and worries.

Belief in Judgment Day can also discourage individuals from violating moral norms and committing transgressions due to fear of being punished in the future. Belief in Heaven and Hell has complementary effects on well-being, creating a balance of forces between individuals' well-being and that of the collective. While beliefs linked to the expectation of reward and happiness in Heaven generate positive feelings that contribute to individual well-being, belief in Hell and the possibility of punishment may seem distressing to individuals at first; in the end, it actually helps curb certain social behaviors, thus protecting collective well-being (Al-Issa et al., 2021). Belief in life after death has a connection with happiness and well-being. According to the Prophet Muhammad (ﷺ):

> Whoever is focused only on this world, Allah will confound his affairs and make him fear poverty constantly, and he will not get anything of this world except that which has been decreed for him. Whoever is focused on the Hereafter, Allah will settle his affairs for him and make him feel content with his lot, and his provision and worldly gains will undoubtedly come to him. (Sunan Ibn Majah)

This Ḥadīth teaches that attachment to worldly life increases yearning and fear of scarcity, while belief in an eternal afterlife reduces worldly expectations and the insatiable search for material happiness. The incessant search for increasing and diverse pleasures is a characteristic of hedonic adaptation, which often leads the subject to believe that we can maximize pleasure. Studies like Roets et al.'s (2012) show that the difficulty in accepting and being content with enough, coupled with the continuous search for better options, ultimately reduces individuals' ability to feel satisfaction and well-being. This logic applies not only to choices related to consumption but also to the ambitions, goals, and desires that individuals build for themselves and the meanings associated with the concept of satisfaction. What are the limits of satisfaction for individual human beings? Does happiness lie in the search for the best or for enough? How can we be satisfied in a world where nothing is permanent and everything is volatile? In Islam, we understand that satisfaction occurs when subjects place their happiness in a future perspective and in a greater spiritual purpose, satisfying themselves with what is enough for them rather than trying to maximize material desires and pleasures of a life that is temporary.

Eternal happiness is the happiness of Paradise, which Muslims hope to achieve as a reward for their actions, sacrifices, and abdications in worldly life. It is the happiness that will be enjoyed in Paradise, so it is an expectation that will be fulfilled in the afterlife. Various terms can be used to name it, such as eternal happiness, happiness in the afterlife, success, triumph, happiness in the other world/in the other life, or transcendental/supernatural happiness, the meaning of which refers to something elevated, sublime, and intangible in human nature. The happiness expected in eternal life is described in the Quran as lasting and permanent: "But you prefer the life of this world, even though the Hereafter is far better and more lasting." (Quran, 87:16–17, interpretation of the meaning).

The Quran is full of verses that characterize life after death. One of the main characteristics of eternal happiness in Paradise is plenitude and complete satisfaction. Not all descriptions of Paradise are understandable to the human mind. The Quran presents it as a transcendental space of great magnitude and perfection, with elements that do not exist in earthly life. Paradise is characterized by terms and expressions referring to a scenario of infinite possibilities for gratification, abundance, beauty, peace, joy, and comfort, without inconvenience, disappointment, or problems. These are attractive descriptions that create strong and unlimited positive expectations. Muslims' greatest expectation of happiness in the afterlife is to be close to Allah (Joshanloo, 2017). Belief in a future life is an inviting promise, often becoming the only hope left for individuals in the face of worldly life's countless evils. That belief creates a strong bond, convincing the person that, like everything else in life, some effort is required to enjoy these rewards. This effort, represented by obedience to divine rules, is the condition under which individuals agree to submit in search of a future goal.

The Quran also provides descriptions of Hell as a place of punishment. In describing the contrast between Paradise and Hell, the Quran relates:

> The description of the Paradise promised to the righteous is that in it are rivers of fresh water, rivers of milk that never changes in taste, rivers of wine delicious to drink, and rivers of pure honey. There they will ʿalsoʾ have all kinds of fruit, and forgiveness from their Lord. ʿCan they beʾ like those who will stay in the Fire forever, left to drink boiling water that will tear apart their insides? (Quran, 47:15, interpretation of the meaning)

Belief in life after death is anchored in the duality between reward and punishment, in the expectation of just and great compensation for all the difficulties, efforts, and good deeds done, or punishment for misdeeds. In fact, this prospect of happiness only suits those who believe in its existence and in the divine promise. Questioning its existence is tantamount to questioning all religious belief, since all these elements are closely intertwined. Wahab (2022) argues that rejecting belief in the invisible, in an afterlife, just because it is not something that can be materially proven, is not an appropriate argument. Over the centuries, science has restricted itself to studying the material and empirical world, ignoring the transcendental and spiritual domain simply because we cannot prove its existence.

References

Ağılkaya-Şahin, Z. (2024). Islamic practices as psychotherapeutic interventions. In C. M. York (Ed.), *Heartfulness: Islamic spiritual practices for health and wellbeing* (pp. 52–83). Alkaram Press.

Abū Dāwūd. Riyad as-Salihin, Hādīth 628. Sunnah.com. https://sunnah.com/riyadussalihin:628

Ahaddour, C., & Broeckaert, B. (2018). "For Every Illness There is a Cure": Attitudes and beliefs of Moroccan Muslim women regarding health, illness and medicine. *Journal of Religion and Health, 57*, 1285–1303. https://doi.org/10.1007/s10943-017-0466-1

Al-Attas, S. M. N. (1995). *Prolegomena to the metaphysics of Islam an exposition of the fundamental elements of the worldview of Islam*. International Institute of Islamic Thought and Civilization (ISTAC).

Alawneh, S. F. (2022). Human motivation: An Islamic perspective. In A. Haque & Y. Mohamed (Eds.), *Psychology of personality: Islamic perspectives* (pp. 175–193). International Association of Islamic Psychology.

Ali, S. S. (2015). The Quranic morality: An introduction to the moral-system of Quran. *Islam and Muslim Societies: A Social Science Journal, 8*(1), 94–108. https://muslimsocieties.org/Vol8_1/The_Quranic_Morality.pdf

Al-Issa, R. S., Krauss, S. E., Roslan, S., & Abdullah, H. (2021). The relationship between after-life beliefs and mental wellbeing among Jordanian Muslim youth. *Journal of Muslim Mental Health, 15*(1), 1–18. https://doi.org/10.3998/jmmh.125

Al-Kaysi, M. I. (2003). *Morals and manners in Islam: A guide to Islamic Adab.* The Islamic Foundation.

Aristóteles. (2003). *Ética a Nicômaco.* Martin Claret.

Atkinson, Q. D., & Bourrat, P. (2011). Beliefs about god, the afterlife and morality support the role of supernatural policing in human cooperation. *Evolution and Human Behavior, 32*(1), 41–49. https://doi.org/10.1016/j.evolhumbehav.2010.07.008

Bakhtiar, L. (2019). *Quranic psychology of the self: A text book on Islamic moral psychology.* Kazi Publications.

Ellison, C. G., Burdette, A. M., & Hill, T. D. (2009). Blessed assurance: Religion, anxiety, and tranquillity among US adults. *Social Science Research, 38*(3), 656–667. https://doi.org/10.1016/j.ssresearch.2009.02.002

Flannelly, K. J., Koenig, H. G., Ellison, C. G., Galek, K., & Krause, N. (2006). Belief in life after death and mental health: Findings from a national survey. *The Journal of Nervous and Mental Disease, 194*(7), 524–529. https://doi.org/10.1097/01.nmd.0000224876.63035.23

Ghauri, M. T. (2011). Religious motivation: A multiplying force. *The Dialogue, 6*(2), 103–123. https://qurtuba.edu.pk/thedialogue/The%20Dialogue/6_2/Dialogue_April_June2011_103-123.pdf

Ihsan, N. H., Huringiin, N., & Indah, N. (2023). Iman as the foundation of Akhlaq in the phenomenon of modern life: Analysis of Said Nursi's thought on Akhlaq. *Tajdid: Jurnal Ilmu Ushuluddin, 22*(1), 102–134. https://doi.org/10.30631/tjd.v22i1.324

Iskandar, J. I. (2012). Avicenna (Ibn Sīnā - 980-1037) and the metaphysical argument for the unity of God in the hermeneutics of the Qur'an. *Trans/Form/Ação (Marília), 35,* 31–42. https://doi.org/10.1590/S0101-31732012000400004.

Joshanloo, M. (2013). A comparison of western and Islamic conceptions of happiness. *Journal of Happiness Studies, 14*(6), 1857–1874. https://doi.org/10.1007/s10902-012-9406-7

Joshanloo, M. (2017). Islamic conceptions of well-being. In R. Estes & M. Sirgy (Eds.), *The pursuit of human well-being. International handbooks of quality-of-life.* Springer. https://doi.org/10.1007/978-3-319-39101-4_5

Joshanloo, M., & Weijers, D. (2019). Islamic perspectives on wellbeing. In L. Lambert & N. Pasha-Zaidi (Eds.), *Positive psychology in the Middle East/North Africa.* Springer. https://doi.org/10.1007/978-3-030-13921-6_11

Kadhim, A. S., Ahmad, S. B., Owoyemi, M. Y., & Ahmad, M. (2017). Islamic ethics: The attributes of Al-Ihsan in the Quran and its effects on Muslim morality. *International Journal of Business and Social Science, 8*(11), 2219–1933. https://www.academia.edu/45627661/Islamic_Ethics_The_Attributes_of_Al_Ihsan_in_the_Quran_and_Its_Effects_on_Muslim_Morality

Kasule, O. H. (2004). *Islamic medical education resources – Islam, Iman, & Ihsan.* Omarkasule. https://omarkasule.tripod.com/id23.html

Mazloum, A. O. (2010). *Passos no Caminho da Felicidade.* Qualitymark.

Muhsin, S. M. (2022). *Iman (Faith), Islam (Submission), Ihsan (Soulful Excellence): Ethical Foundations in Islam.* Islamonweb. https://en.Islamonweb.net/Iman-faith-Islam-submission-i%E1%B8%A5san-soulful-excellence-ethical-foundations-in-Islam

Munsoor, M. S. (2021). *Wellbeing and the worshipper.* Springer.

Muslim. Ḥadīth 2, 40 Ḥadīth an-Nawawi. Sunnah.com. https://sunnah.com/nawawi40:2.

Mustaffa, N. H., & Akhir, N. S. M. (2019). The concept of Saʿādah according to Islamic, Western, and Greek views. *European Proceedings of Social and Behavioural Sciences.* https://doi.org/10.15405/epsbs.2020.10.02.8

Nabi, U. (2024). Akhlāq and subjective well-being: Exploring the mediating role of perceived stress using structural equation modelling. *Social Sciences & Humanities Open, 10,* 101000. https://doi.org/10.1016/j.ssaho.2024.101000

Nasr, S. H. (2014). Happiness and the attainment of happiness: An Islamic perspective. *Journal of Law and Religion, 29*(01), 76–91. https://doi.org/10.1017/jlr.2013.18

Omais, S., & dos Santos, M. A. (2022). Happiness in Islam: The role of religion and spirituality in Muslims' well-being. In N. N. M. Shariff, M. A. Yakob, Z. S. Hamidi, Z. A. A. Aghwan, & N. Lateh (Eds.), *Selected Proceedings from the 1st International Conference on Contemporary Islamic Studies (ICIS 2021)* (pp. 207–215). Springer.

Omais, S., Tarif, E., & Santos, M. A. (2023). Ethics, morals, virtues and character strengths: A comparison between Islamic psychology and positive psychology. In C. Y. Al-Karam (Ed.), *The way of love* (pp. 129–152). Al Karam Press.

Roets, A., Schwartz, B., & Guan, Y. (2012). The tyranny of choice: A cross-cultural investigation of maximizing-satisficing effects on well-being. *Judgment and Decision Making, 7*(6), 689–704. https://doi.org/10.1017/S1930297500003247

Sabjan, M. A. (2019). The meaning and experience of happiness in Islam: An overview. *The European Proceedings of Social & Behavioural Sciences.* The Second International Conference on Humanities.

Saleam, J., & Moustafa, A. A. (2016). The influence of divine rewards and punishments on religious prosociality. *Frontiers in Psychology, 7,* 1149. https://doi.org/10.3389/fpsyg.2016.01149

Saritoprak, S. N., & Abu-Raiya, H. (2023). Living the good life: An Islamic perspective on positive psychology. In E. B. Davis, E. L. Worthington Jr., & S. A. Schnitker (Eds.), *Handbook of positive psychology, religion, and spirituality* (pp. 197–194). Springer. https://doi.org/10.1007/978-3-031-10274-5_12

Sunan Ibn Majah. Book 37, Vol. 5, Ḥadīth 4105. Sunnah.com. https://sunnah.com/ibnmajah:4105

Tajul Ariffin, A. H., AbdulKhaiyom, J. H., & Rosli, A. N. (2022). Islam, Iman, and Ihsan: The role of religiosity on quality of life and mental health of Muslim undergraduate students. *IIUM Medical Journal Malaysia, 21*(3), 146–154. https://doi.org/10.31436/imjm.v21i3.2047

The Clear Quran. (n.d.). (M. Khattab, Trans.). https://Quran.com/

Utz, A. (2011). *Psychology from Islamic perspective.* International Islamic Publishing House.

Wahab, M. A. (2022). Islamic spiritual and emotional intelligence and its relationship to eternal happiness: A conceptual paper. *Journal of Religion and Health, 61*(6), 4783–4806. https://doi.org/10.1007/s10943-021-01485-2

Wiliasih, R., Siregar, H., Irawan, T., & Beik, I. S. (2024). Happiness in Islam and Influencing Factors (SLR Approach). *AL-MUZARA'AH - Journal of Islamic Economics & Finance, 12*(1), 137–157. https://doi.org/10.29244/jam.12.1.137-157

Chapter 5
Islamic Conceptions of the Human Psyche and Psychospiritual Well-Being

Studies on subjective well-being (SWB) have been widely disseminated in the literature in recent years, but these are limited to a particular worldview, and there is a shortage of measuring instruments that specifically align with Islamic concepts and values. In order to compare Western and Islamic well-being scales, some authors found that the concept of subjective well-being (SWB) and Islamic well-being (IWB) have differences, but also common ground.

Because it is a totally spiritual concept built on the foundations of religion since its revelation, the Islamic concept of happiness is unchanging over time, and its true meaning derives from guidelines established by God. These teachings are based on a timeless idea of happiness and not a generational or momentary construct, linked to changes in society that constantly create new desires, turning consumption into happiness's main currency. Hence, we find the importance of investigating the Quran and other Islamic sources in order to better understand the factors relevant to well-being in the view of this population. The following topics discuss some differences between the Western perspective and the Islamic perspective of well-being, based on theoretical models and studies present in the literature.

5.1 Western and Islamic Conceptions of Well-Being

From the Islamic perspective, Muslims believe that God is Omnipotent and Omniscient, Creator of the Universe and humanity. There would be no one better than Him to guide humans on the real path to happiness, since they can have their rationality overshadowed and be easily seduced by hedonism, momentary gratifications, and unrealistic expectations. Because it is a concept of happiness that comes from external guidance and not just from rationality, subjective evaluations, or a purely human value judgment, in Islam, the objective element of happiness ends up taking precedence over subjective well-being (Joshanloo & Weijers, 2019).

S. Omais, *Happiness and Well-Being in Islam*,
https://doi.org/10.1007/978-3-031-95353-8_5

Differences observed by Eryilmaz and Kula (2020) between the Western and Islamic perspectives of well-being focus precisely on the fact that the former is constructed without adapting to Muslim values, beliefs, and understanding of well-being.

To better understand the basis of well-being in Islam, we need to understand the meaning of obedience and submission. It is the starting point for understanding this issue from an Islamic perspective, since this theme is one of the foundations of a Muslim's psychospiritual well-being. Obedience to divine precepts allows believers to have a clear conscience about their self (psychological well-being) and their relationship with God (spiritual well-being), even if this implies individuals giving up certain things.

In Islam, obedience to God is considered the highest virtue a human being can have (Nasr, 2008). Here, we must draw attention to the great contrast between Islamic values and Western/secular values. While in the West, obedience and submission are perceived as forms of humiliation, oppression of human freedom, and conduct that denotes immaturity and ignorance, in Islam it is exactly the opposite. Obedience to God is not only a virtue but the greatest of them all. Humility is the first virtue needed for someone to agree to submit. Submission and obedience are attitudes that require humans to admit their limitations, vulnerabilities, imperfections, and inability to be self-sufficient. Superimposing human will on divine will is a symbol of creation's ingratitude to, and arrogance about, its Creator. It disrespects divine wisdom, His omniscience, and His authority. It is precisely in this contrast of values that the West's antagonism and resistance to Islam lie. In the West, human decisions are basically "human," whereas in Islam, human decisions are directed by divine commands and Prophetic teachings. Obedience is an act of humility on the part of human beings before the One who created them and His Omnipotence. Muslims' relationship with God is not one of competition or confrontation, but simply one of submission. And this submission only occurs if there is total trust in God's existence and in His Wisdom in every aspect.

This is why the idea of happiness and well-being in Islam is connected to the very reality and nature of life, starting from a concept that is more objective than subjective. Reducing it solely to human subjectivity can lead humans into error, to illusory expectations, and to the illusion often created by the sense organs and by their impulsive and immediate nature. This often makes them susceptible to wrong perceptions and assessments about what is good or bad for them. The concept of subjectivity focuses all decisions, interpretations, perceptions, cognitive evaluations, emotions, and behaviors on the individual. However, although psychological science focuses on this concept, we must understand that, depending on the cultural perspective, this subjectivity may not play a central role in the subject's decisions and behaviors. This exclusive focus on subjectivity actually stems from a psychology built around an individual and secular perspective, where the human being is the center of everything.

By using the concept of submission and obedience as a foundation in Islam, individuals and their subjectivity cease to be the sole center of decisions, interpretations, and evaluations. This is because they begin to follow a set of external spiritual guidelines that override their ability to discern right and wrong, good and bad. This logic is reinforced by the verse that says: "Perhaps you dislike something which is good for you and like something which is bad for you. Allah knows and you do not know" (Quran, 2:216).

According to Ibn Kathir (Quran.com, n.d.), this verse reinforces that only God has exact knowledge of what will benefit human beings in their worldly or eternal life. This passage from the Quran reveals that everything in life can be relative, both the good and the bad. In other words, submission and obedience are an act in which subjects give up their subjectivity to follow directions from without that they fully trust. Therefore, obedience to divine commands and guidance is more reliable and safer for Muslims than their limited capacity for evaluation.

The intrinsic motivation leading Muslims to obey God can be positive, inspired by love for God, or negative, due to fear of punishment. Fear of divine punishment represents the initial stage of submission, in which people repent and strive to change their behavior to avoid pain and punishment. From this point on, they broaden their consciousness and take responsibility for their actions. As they go through trials during life, they understand that disobedience to God and His rules is the path to worry, misery, sadness, and unhappiness, both in this life and the next. When individuals obey God and His rules only out of love for Him, they reach a higher level of spirituality, a stage where they no longer need coercion, fear, or awe. It is simply love for God that guides their actions. Fear may be necessary in the beginning when individuals are still spiritually immature and do not act spontaneously but are driven by the search for a reward or fear of punishment (Wahab, 2022). For Joshanloo (2013), fear leads individuals to a more complete submission. As they evolve, they begin to understand the goodness, mercy, and love of God, and start to act out of that feeling alone. Individuals do not stop believing in divine punishment and wrath, but only change the motivation behind their actions (Wahab, 2022).

Although a worldly life guided by divine rules or *Shariah* does not guarantee a perfect, financially prosperous life—free from problems or challenges—it allows individuals to be better prepared to serenely face life's setbacks. Not least because Islam's focus is on spiritual rather than material progress, although nothing prevents Muslims from achieving both. This is yet another reason why the Islamic view of well-being is not linked to pleasure or happiness per se, as Muslims believe that adversities can also be beneficial to individuals. Emotions, therefore, do not serve as a reference point for well-being (Joshanloo, 2017; Joshanloo & Weijers, 2019). Hence, all individuals have a way of interpreting the facts of life and experience emotions of different types and intensities, which makes subjectivity an unstable and imprecise element for measuring well-being. This explains why some authors criticize the universal measurement instruments that exist today. These well-being indicators, wrongly considered "universal" by science, based on the Western worldview, more often than not do not include Muslims' religiosity and spirituality in a deep manner, and when they do, it is usually done superficially (Joshanloo & Weijers, 2019).

Worldly existence is imperfect by nature for each and every human being. Even if brief moments of joy or a "good" life exist, Joshanloo (2017) states that we cannot achieve genuine and lasting happiness in worldly life, as suffering and difficulties are inherent in it. Muslims remain faithful to the teachings because they believe that both good times and bad times in life are part of the divine plan, and both are spiritual tests aimed at strengthening their faith. Islam teaches that faith must be unconditional and independent of the blessings or tribulations that individuals experience, since not every evil necessarily represents a punishment.

Religiosity and spirituality are the main focus of the Islamic conception of well-being. This is not simply an "extra" or "complementary" element, as seen in the Western secular perspective, but rather the main basis that coordinates and guides all other elements. Eryilmaz and Kula (2020) highlight two aspects that explain the relationship between well-being and religion in Muslims' lives (Fig. 5.1). One is based on individuals' own interpretations of happiness, which is a subjective characteristic similar to the concept of subjective well-being. The second aspect, on the other hand, is where happiness is perceived and internalized from the divine narratives and guidelines present in religious scriptures. It is at this point that spiritual teachings influence well-being, causing even negative situations to be reframed and assimilated positively.

Eryilmaz and Kula (2020) also recall that there is a more moderate hedonism in Islam, marked by human needs related to pleasures that, like eudaimonic happiness, are also considered important for Muslims' lives, as long as they do not exceed the limits and conditions established by doctrine. Therefore, the subjective concept of happiness depends directly on the objective concept, because lack of alignment of actions and behaviors with religious precepts can interfere directly with the Muslim feeling of well-being. This would only cease to occur the moment that the religious and transcendental element ceases to be important in people's lives and personal satisfaction becomes their sole and main criterion for happiness. This trajectory marked the emergence of societies adhering to the process of secularization. It replaced the space previously occupied by religion with human discretion and a conception of well-being centered on individuals, their wishes, and their own judgment.

Thus, if well-being from a Quranic perspective would be a life where actions and intentions are all focused on worship and obedience to God, then the fundamental

Fig. 5.1 The influence of religious orientations on subjective well-being according to Eryilmaz and Kula (2020)—Adapted by the author

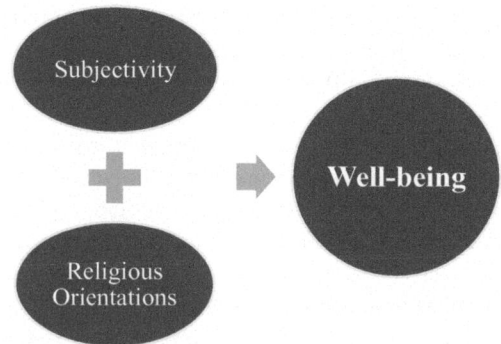

basis for this construct in Islam would, above all, be in spirituality, in an objective conception of happiness linked to divine commands and not in rationality, nor in sensations, emotions, or in the frequency of positive subjective experiences. According to Joshanloo (2017), subjective states in this case would be the product of this objective dimension, that is, of spiritual dedication, mastery over the lower self, and virtuous behavior, because it is from this that people are able to have a real and lasting sense of well-being, characterized by feelings of tranquility, security, and contentment (Fig. 5.2). This would be ideal happiness in Islam, which, in fact, is closer to the eudaimonic perspective. Feelings of peace and contentment also derive from individuals' acceptance of and satisfaction with divine designs that end up reducing worry and anxiety about what they have no control over.

Thus, contrary to the Western perspective, positive emotions are not the central point of well-being for Muslims, but rather it is moral and religious awareness of their actions, even though many morally correct behaviors may, at first, displease the individual (Fig. 5.3). An act of generosity, for example, involving material donations, may initially arouse fear of losing part of one's wealth or frustration at having to give away something important to someone else. However, trust in God and the hope that all one's efforts will be rewarded, whether in this worldly life or after death, override these feelings in the end.

Cognition, connected to religious teachings, influences individuals' emotions. Therefore, if emotions vary according to the processing of information, both positive and negative emotions become relative. This is because, under the lens of religious teachings, the redefinition and interpretation of facts can change individuals' perception and evaluation of their feelings and their lives, both positively and negatively, depending on whether or not their actions are aligned with Islamic precepts. Individuals' evaluation of their lives, although subjective, can be made based on cultural and religious beliefs or on their own perceptions. It may be difficult to say that individuals are capable of isolating the beliefs and values absorbed throughout life from their own perceptions and sensations. These subjective perceptions,

Fig. 5.2 Objective and subjective dimensions of well-being in Islam according to Joshanloo (2017)—Adapted by the author

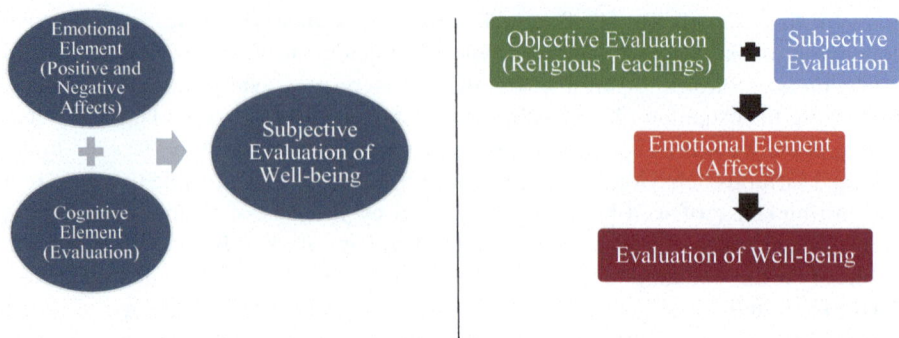

Fig. 5.3 Difference between the subjective well-being of Diener's Tripartite Model (1984) and the Islamic well-being concept—Adapted by the author

however, may clash with their own beliefs at certain times, or even a conflict between religious beliefs and sociocultural influences may also lead to confusion.

In the case of Islam, Muslims are instructed to expand this perception to a broader dimension that is not based solely on immediate emotions or sensations, or on the first impression that comes to mind, since what seems obvious or explicit can often be illusory. Based on the premise that it is illogical for a creature to know the paths to happiness better than its Creator, which is how Islam also understands it, hence we have the need to be guided by religious knowledge. Muslims comprehend that the search for happiness does not always lie in what appears to be better or more pleasurable to human eyes, since the senses can be deceptive and their ability to discern this is often limited, contrary to their Creator's guidance. To better illustrate this limitation, we can think of a situation where someone loses his or her job, evaluating such an event as negative at first. This is the most immediate and even the only subjective perception of the fact. However, when adding the religious idea that this loss may generate some future benefit that they are still unaware of, their cognitive assessment, as well as their emotional reaction, may change.

Islam warns Muslims that not everything appearing to be good is entirely good, just as not everything that appears to be bad is entirely bad. This limitation of the human mind in evaluating facts in their entirety makes both positive and negative dimensions important for well-being. The most immediate emotions and sensations can harm individuals' evaluations if they are based on negative and positive feelings or on a purely subjective value judgment, which is based solely on their perception of reality. Therefore, Islamic teachings serve as a guide for Muslims, instructing them to interpret facts not in their explicit form, in the way they appear to be, but rather in the implicit aspects that are often hidden beneath such situations and that are not always correctly evaluated at first glance or immediately understood. Therefore, we cannot always categorize human experiences as positive or negative, good or bad, since all can be relativized from a spiritual perspective, leading individuals directly or indirectly to happiness and well-being. For example, receiving a fortune suddenly can be a blessing and bring a lot of joy to people, but it can also be a negative factor, disrupting their social relationships, changing their attitudes and their way of acting toward others, or even taking them away from the spiritual path. Hence, we see the importance of relativizing how we perceive each life situation rather than giving them absolute interpretations or evaluations that disregard such variables.

When considering that not everything may be as it seems, individuals are encouraged to judge life events cautiously and objectively, using religious teachings as a guide and support for the human intellect. The belief that there is something good in all divine plans, even those that seem bad to us, increases the chances of people feeling satisfied with life because, instead of depositing all their happiness only in "apparently" good moments, they also start to include bad moments as positive ones if interpreted through a spiritual prism.

Thus, unlike subjective well-being, Muslims' assessments are directly influenced by elements linked to their beliefs and not by the relationship between positive and negative feelings. This combination of subjective assessment with the objective element from the Islamic perspective helps subjects interpret facts from different angles, as merely human value judgment is limited to knowledge of what is tangible and explicit to him or her. If human emotions are the result of thought, then beliefs and cognitions formed from religious teachings fashion the basis for a rational understanding of circumstances, influencing the person's process of evaluating life (Fig. 5.3).

Similarly, even though a given situation is bad, religious teachings can make individuals understand it in the opposite way. In addition to contributing to well-being, this is also advantageous for resilience, due to the coping effect that spiritual resignification can have on the way one reacts to life events, reflecting positively on the individual's emotional state. However, for this to be possible, individuals must, first of all, necessarily have the pillars of faith well crystallized to establish their relationship of trust in God, His teachings, and the divine plan.

5.2 Islamic Conceptions and Theoretical Models of the Human Psyche and Psychospiritual Well-Being

One of well-being's characteristics is emotional balance, which is influenced by several elements. Psychospiritual balance in Islam results from the dynamics of the soul's four elements and the stages individuals go through as they evolve spiritually until reaching a state of spiritual and psychological well-being. Although most studies of the soul use Al-Ghazali's knowledge as a starting point, some have proposed models with different conceptions of the psyche's dynamics. Following Al-Ghazālī's teachings, various authors have constructed and refined interpretations of the self by tracing the relationships between elements of the soul and mental health and well-being.

It is, therefore, essential to understand the models that explain the human psyche's internal dynamics from an Islamic perspective in order to draw hypotheses about well-being. Thus, this section discusses some of the theories and models that explain internal functioning and the elements that can interfere positively or negatively in this dynamic, as well as others that speak more specifically about the factors that can contribute to happiness and well-being from an Islamic perspective.

We should note that some authors refer to internal processes as the dynamics of the self, while others use the term "soul." These terms still appear mixed together in many studies in the area. The word "soul," however, encompasses much more than traditional psychic functions. Soul is a broader concept. In Islam, although it sometimes refers to the element that gives life to the body, or to behavioral inclinations, or to the spiritual heart, it also has a more global dimension that encompasses the combination of all these elements and the functions that make up the psyche or the self. Our intention here is not to invalidate the use of the term self or psyche to describe psychological processes specifically. However, just as the body is used in a global way to describe the elements that make it up and the physiological processes, the existence of spiritual elements that interact with psychic functions also requires the use of a nomenclature that accommodates the Islamic psychospiritual conception more completely. Thus, preference is given to the term "soul."

5.2.1   The Islamic Model of the Self

The Islamic paradigm of psychology is completely centered on God and His teachings, which is why Skinner (2018) defines mental health as a state in which the *qalb*, under divine inspiration from the *rūḥ*, is able to control the self (*nafs*) by aligning it with its pure and divine nature (*fitrah*). The Islamic model of the self proposed by Rasjid Skinner (2018) aimed at facilitating and guiding the diagnosis and clinical treatment of patients based on the relationships between the heart (*qalb*), the intellect (*aql*), the animal or instinctive self (*hawa*), and the body. He explains that the *qalb* is the place where we find the *fitrah*, the sense of right and wrong, and it is guided by the spirit (*rūḥ*) through dreams or inspirations. Following Al-Ghazali's teachings, Skinner reveals that the intellect (*aql*) carries five operational attributions, four of which are related to logical functions. The fifth, a function articulating the intellect with the wisdom of the heart (*qalb*), will guide the other intellectual functions to prevent them from straying from the *fitrah*, that is, from the path of righteousness and purity. The *aql* would therefore be comparable to a horse's reins, represented by the animal self (*hawa*), guided by the rider, represented by the heart (*qalb*) connected to God through the spirit (*rūḥ*) in order to guide him or her toward the spiritual path. Skinner's ideas attempt to explain better and expand upon some of Al-Ghazālī's ideas for understanding the soul's dynamic, although the theory can still be expanded.

5.2.2 The Causality Model of the Elements of the Human Psyche

Al-Ghazali's theory advocated that holistic mental well-being would result from the harmonious relationship among the four elements of the soul: *rūḥ, qalb, nafs,* and *aql*. This relationship, according to Keshavarzi and Haque (2013), is regulated by divine guidance present in three major Islamic sciences: religious creed (*aqeedah*), external behavior that implies obedience to Islamic norms and jurisprudence (*fiqh*), and the refinement of character (*akhlaq*) that develops through spirituality (*tassawuf*).

One of the elements that influences human well-being is the cognitive interpretation the person gives to external sensory stimuli (Keshavarzi & Keshavarzi, 2021). Yusuf and Elhaddad (2020) emphasize that the intellect (*aql*) is decisive for well-being and mental health, both for its ability to resignify maladaptive thoughts and for the individual's process of internal moral transformation. Through this logic, emotion would be a product derived from cognitive evaluation (*aql*). Therefore, spiritual and cultural beliefs and subjective experiences, as well as several other factors, can directly influence people's emotional state. Using Al-Ghazali's psycho-ethical model, the authors explain that the cognition–emotion–behavior relationship is not a linear process. The activation of any one of them can influence the other elements, regardless of which is activated first. Another fundamental element linked to the intellect is conscience (*insishaf*). This is the starting point for individuals to reflect and realize their flaws in order to reestablish the self's balance.

The *nafs* reflects the individual's behaviors, which, when repeated and excessively inclined toward biological impulses and desires, need to undergo spiritual training to readjust. The *nafs'* inclinations influence individuals' internal emotional balance and can generate different emotions, as occurs during the three stages of the *nafs'* evolution. Actions practiced by the lower self (*nafs al lammarah*), generally inclined toward desire or other impulsive behaviors, can generate feelings of joy, pleasure, or anger. In the state of consciousness, when individuals are confronted by their critical self (*nafs al lawamah*), feelings of shame, fear, guilt, sadness, or regret may arise. In the highest stage, when the self evolves spiritually, reaching the *nafs mutmainah*, the feelings would be of peace, tranquility, and satisfaction (Keshavarzi & Haque, 2013; Keshavarzi & Keshavarzi, 2021).

Psychospiritual health has a close connection to spirituality. Therefore, purification of the heart is linked to the strengthening of spiritual identity (Keshavarzi & Haque, 2013; Keshavarzi & Ali, 2019). Keshavarzi et al. (2021) demonstrate that changes in the spiritual dimension (*rūḥ*) have a broader dimension than those focused on other elements of the soul and can affect different dimensions of individuals' psyche, including under the influence of external transcendental and spiritual elements. One of the ways to strengthen the spirit (*rūḥ*) is through remembrance of God (*dhikr*), a practice that can generate various benefits. Traditional Islamic rituals such as charity, fasting, prayers, pilgrimage, repentance (*tawbah*), and supplication (*duaa*) are also behaviors cited in the literature as options for strengthening spirituality and connection with God. The spirit is linked to meaning, purpose, the sacred, and connection with the divine (Keshavarzi & Khan, 2018).

In the Islamic view, the heart (*qalb*) is the human psyche's central structure. For Al-Ghazali, the heart is where the effects of the soul's other structures are manifested, which is why it is understood that when it becomes ill, the entire body becomes ill, as stated in Prophetic sayings. The heart's health is reestablished, according to Keshavarzi and Haque (2013), through a change in the *nafs'* inclinations toward the practice of good conduct, an intellect (*aql*) aligned with the moral norms of Islam, and a strengthened spirit (*rūḥ*) through the remembrance of God. The authors explain that interventions in any of the three elements, *nafs, aql,* or *rūḥ*, have a positive impact on the others, thus contributing to the health of the heart (*qalb*). A few years later, Keshavarzi and Khan (2018) added one more element: emotion (*ihsaas*). While some consider emotion an implicit element in the sphere represented by the heart (*qalb*) or the spirit (*rūḥ*), as a complement to Al-Ghazali's theory, the authors include emotions as a separate element due to the emphasis this theme is given in the literature.

The authors also emphasize the importance of the social context (*ijtima'i*) for the integration of the psyche's elements, since human beings are naturally interrelational creatures and interconnected with the environment around them. They explain that the interaction of the human psyche's elements, *nafs, aql, ihsaas,* and *rūḥ*, both internally and with the social environment and/or the physical environment—that is, the treatment given by individuals to their peers or to other dimensions of divine creation, such as nature—is also part of human beings' spiritual growth, internally influencing people. Therefore, there is a constant emphasis in the literature on a more holistic and integrated view to understand human dynamics.

5.2.3 The Islamic Model of the Soul

The model proposed by Rothman and Coyle (2018) describes the dynamics of the soul's four elements mentioned in the Quran (*nafs, rūḥ, qalb,* and *aql*), readapting the model suggested by Al-Ghazali. The model describes not only the dynamics among them but also the steps necessary for the person to achieve balance, that is, a state of peace and tranquility. When individuals follow religious precepts and strengthen their connection with God, the clash between the self of desires and impulses (*nafs al amarah*) and the critical self (*nafs al lawamah*) does not occur, or, if it does, the critical self manages to prevail, and individuals then reach the highest level of self (*nafs al mutmainnah*), that of the soul at peace.

Without the spirit's (*rūḥ's*) strong connection with God and a strong intellect (*aql*) connected to the spirit (*rūḥ*) and the heart (*qalb*), the critical self would have greater difficulty in winning this struggle, since the *nafs el amarah's* animalistic desires are strong and intense. This explains the meaning of the expression *nafs el amarah*, which can also be translated as the commanding self, the inferior self, or the self that is inclined to evil.

5.2.3.1   The Model of Spiritual Intelligence and Emotional Intelligence

In the study conducted by Wahab (2022), well-being would be the result of the union between individuals' spiritual intelligence and emotional intelligence (Fig. 5.4). The author also uses Al-Ghazali's spiritual conception to connect spiritual evolution with a better ability to manage emotions. Thus, spiritual intelligence, formed from religious and spiritual knowledge, would be individuals' starting point for individuals to develop their own emotional intelligence, since individuals would only be able to evolve and tame their most primitive instincts through frequent connection with God, combined with love and fear, knowledge, and purification of the soul. Complete dedication to God, anchored by religiosity and spirituality, would form the path to a good life in this life and in eternal life. Therefore, as individuals evolve spiritually, they are able to have greater control and management of their impulses, reducing these internal conflicts. According to Wahab (2022), evolution through the three stages of the soul, from *nafs al-amarah, nafs al-lawammah*, until reaching *nafs al-mutmainnah*, increases individuals' ability to distinguish between good and evil, to tame their impulses, to balance their emotions, and consequently, to perfect their character by practicing virtues. It would be in the last stage, *nafs al-mutmainnah*, that the union of spiritual intelligence with emotional intelligence would occur, since only spiritual evolution would enable people to manage their emotions in a balanced way (Wahab, 2022).

Wahab (2022) highlights that sincere love for God is the decisive factor in Islam for happiness in this world and the next. It is God who guides all of individuals' cognitions and behaviors, protecting them from that which is not beneficial to them. Purifying mistakes through repentance and abstaining from certain acts also generates happiness and a sense of relief. Evil and sins provide human beings only brief moments of pleasure, making individuals dependent on fleeting and insatiable happiness. For traditional science, the discomfort in this case could be related to individuals' beliefs and cognition. From a spiritual perspective, however, this explanation

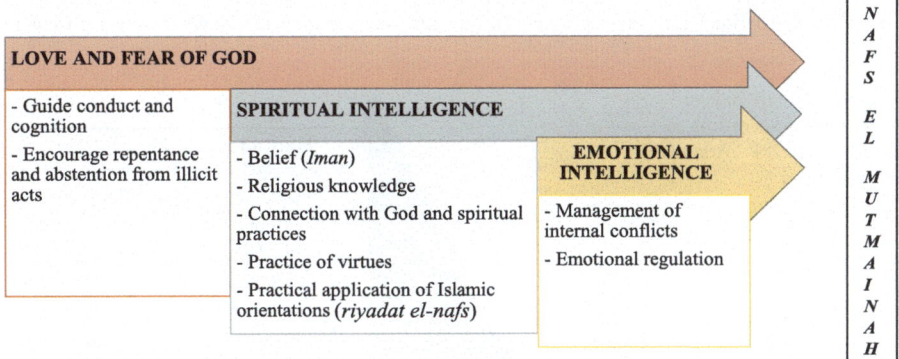

Fig. 5.4 Well-being as a union of spiritual intelligence with emotional intelligence according to Wahab (2022)—Adapted by the author

would be somewhat simplistic, given that bad behavior destabilizes and generates disharmony among individuals' hearts, spirits, intellects, and selves. This imbalance between these internal structures of the soul or psyche can be perceived and felt through bad sensations, discomfort, disconnection, inner emptiness, distress, and malaise. Spiritual intelligence, however, is only possible through continuous training (*riyadat el nafs*), spiritual experience, belief, and practical application of Islamic teachings not only in isolated practices and rituals but in all individuals' acts and behaviors, whether religious or secular. These actions bring individuals closer and strengthen their bond with God, giving them a greater sense of tranquility. The possibility of spiritual evolution, together with the improvement of character and behavior, shows a dynamic and optimistic view of Islam, thus contradicting deterministic versions of psychology that reduce the subject to a permanent and unchanging condition.

5.2.4 Al-Attas' Conception of Happiness

Al-Attas' ideas about happiness in Islam are directly related to the Qur'anic concept discussed in the previous chapter. According to Al-Attas (1995), the ultimate goal of happiness in Islam is love directed at God. The author reveals the existence of three levels of happiness, two of which are in worldly life and the last in the afterlife (Fig. 5.5). The first level is temporary and psychological, linked to the emotions and feelings generated when human beings manage to satisfy their needs and desires in a correct, lawful, and virtuous way. This worldly happiness is more linked to material or bodily desires and has a characteristic more connected to hedonism. The second level of happiness is spiritual, which, unlike the first, is more lasting, experienced through consciousness, where individuals see worldly life as a probationary stage, preventing them from becoming vain about achievements and shaken by life's hardships. At this level, individuals are strengthened by virtuous behavior, which gradually generates satisfaction and helps reduce desires. If this level is achieved together with the first, individuals' needs are satisfied, and there is a reduction in

Fig. 5.5 The three levels of happiness according to Al-Attas (1995)—Adapted by the author

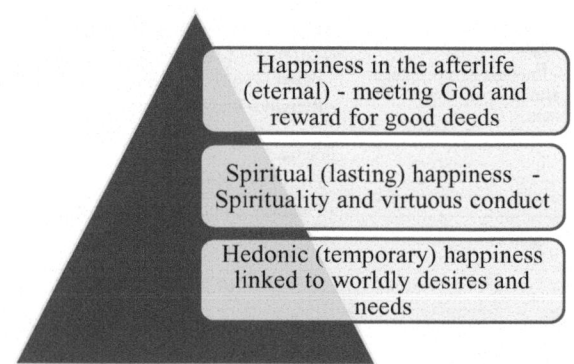

Happiness in the afterlife (eternal) - meeting God and reward for good deeds

Spiritual (lasting) happiness - Spirituality and virtuous conduct

Hedonic (temporary) happiness linked to worldly desires and needs

worldly desires. This second level would be the preparatory stage to reaching the third and final level, that of eternal happiness after death, where individuals will be rewarded for their actions and efforts and have their long-awaited encounter with God (Al-Attas, 1995).

Although there is a consensus among several authors in Islamic psychology about Islam's holistic nature, as of yet, there are few models in the literature that illustrate the connection among well-being's various facets. This is actually a challenging task, as it is a topic that simultaneously integrates several fields of knowledge. As Islamic behavior also has this integrated perspective, separating each element and uniting them in a single model is not an easy or definitive task. There are countless possibilities to illustrate the connection between Islamic teachings, the elements that make up the human personality, and the different areas of life. Some models focus more on the cognitive aspect, others concentrate on the different dimensions of the self and personality, while others bring an integrated view with other areas of life.

5.2.5 The Positive Psychology Model Based on the Islamic Paradigm of Optimism

Optimism plays a central role in studies on well-being, as it has a direct relationship with the emotional state and the way in which individuals interpret life events. Several Islamic teachings reinforce this optimistic perspective. In their study, Khodayarifard et al. (2016) suggest an Islamic perspective of positive psychology focused on the construct of positive thinking. These authors connect positive beliefs and cognitions to an ontological view of Islam in light of attachment theory, starting from the principle that strong and secure attachments result in individuals who are more optimistic, resilient, hopeful, and have more positive expectations regarding the future and the people around them. This is unlike those with insecure attachment who, in the end, develop anxious, avoidant behaviors and feelings of worthlessness. Such characteristics would be enhanced by spiritual beliefs that favor agency, motivating individuals to act and deal better with certain situations. The positive view of humans in Islam, combined with gratitude, belief in compassion and divine kindness, and trust in God (*tawakkul*), are some of the spiritual teachings these authors cite that give individuals a more optimistic view of themselves, God, and others around them. They point out two dimensions related to optimism in their model. The first is the dimension related to time, that is, it is individuals' ability to interpret facts from the past, present, and future with a positive bias. The second would be the relational dimension, which reflects individuals' ability to think positively and optimistically about four types of relationships: in the relationship with oneself, believing in one's abilities and qualities; in the relationship with others, focusing on the best in other people; in the relationship with nature, admiring the grandeur and perfection of divine creation; and in the relationship with God, developing a bond of trust in God, in His compassion, and in the wisdom of divine plans.

Individuals' surrender to divine will only occurs based on a positive view of God and a strong bond of trust between individuals and their Creator. The authors explain that this trust and positive perception of God, of His Presence at all times, and of His Omnipotence provide a secure attachment and a stable base for individuals that provide them with solidity, support, and feelings of peace and tranquility. Belief in omnipresence and divine protection at any time and in any place reduces feelings of helplessness and insecurity and strengthens hope and optimism in individuals, even in the face of challenging situations. The Quran illustrates this context when it states, "And whoever puts their trust in Allāh, then He is sufficient for them. Certainly Allāh achieves His Will" (Quran, 65:3). The Islamic religion shows an optimistic perspective on human beings and their capacity for evolution. This paradigm, which includes the vision of God, the individual himself, and his peers, would be decisive for human well-being and thriving.

5.2.6 The Multidimensional Model of the Self (Descriptive-Normative Model)

In Faruque's model (2021), soul training and spiritual evolution are considered a way of "sculpting the self." According to him, the self (*nafs*) is susceptible to negative personality traits such as envy, pride, and arrogance. These characteristics encourage people to satisfy desires linked to their body or ego that guarantee some superiority over other people. The author suggests a descriptive-normative model of well-being. The descriptive dimension includes the biopsychological, sociocultural, and cognitive-experiential factors of the self, and the normative dimension encompasses the ethical self and the spiritual self.

On the one hand, what the author presents are basically acquired factors that are already part of the personality, and on the other, factors that can be developed or improved by the person. Thus, the descriptive dimension encompasses elements already present in the individual's self, formed from biological, cultural, social, and cognitive factors accumulated throughout life. The normative dimension represents the part of the self that seeks to evolve and improve itself. These are the aspirations that help lead people from the current disturbed state in which they find themselves to an ideal stage of internal transformation. This normative dimension is more focused on self-knowledge, philosophical reflections, spiritual exercises, and the practice of virtues.

5.2.7   The Well-Being Model Inspired by the Teachings and Life of the Prophet Muhammad (ﷺ)

The Prophet Muhammad's (ﷺ) trajectory was marked by a series of teachings and spiritual guidance regarding various aspects of human life. It was through his conduct and recommendations, combined with the Quran's precepts, that early Islamic scholars and researchers developed some theories of well-being. Munsoor (2021) illustrates the Prophet Muhammad's (ﷺ) legacy by dividing it into three dimensions: individuals' relationship with God (suprarelationship), individuals' relationship with themselves (intrarelationship), and individuals' relationship with other people (interrelationship). According to the author, this relationship is linked to the effort of the soul (*jihad-el-nafs*) which, in addition to being a path to self-development, differs somewhat from the Western paradigm of well-being.

From this basis, Munsoor (2021) brings together the five main themes included in the Prophetic traditions, which together form a "guide" of instructions divided into five domains of well-being: spiritual, psychological, social, physical, and intellectual. This model reveals a broader conception of well-being that encompasses the different aspects of human life. The intellectual domain encompasses knowledge in its broadest sense, that is, both religious knowledge and that related to divine creation, which helps individuals logically understand the contents and purpose of faith. The author includes each of Islam's pillars in the spiritual dimension, emphasizing the importance of concentration and the quality with which rituals are performed, such as prayer, for example, which requires focused attention (*kushu*). This group also includes the practice of charity, fasting, pilgrimage to Mecca, and other complementary spiritual practices like contemplation and meditation.

Regarding the social aspect and collective welfare, the author brings together Prophetic guidelines related to morality (*akhlaq*), to daily actions (*deen el muamalat*), to the improvement of behaviors, and to the practice of virtues. The physical dimension is guided by a Prophetic model that encourages the pursuit of a healthy body through a moderate and healthy diet and physical exercises, such as those practiced or suggested by the Prophet Muhammad (ﷺ), like martial arts, horseback riding, fencing, archery, swimming, running, and others. Finally, with regard to the psychological domain, Munsoor (2021) includes some mental states practiced and taught by the Prophet (ﷺ), such as consciousness based on fear of God (*taqwa*), the state of contentment (*ridha*), the state of presence, gratitude, and material detachment through a modest life.

5.3 Elements and Requirements That Contribute to Happiness and Well-Being

Understanding the Islamic paradigm of happiness and well-being includes not only knowledge of the processes but also of the factors that contribute to this state. Eryilmaz and Kula (2020) cite three important requirements for happiness from an Islamic perspective (Fig. 5.6). The first requirement would be belief in the pillars of faith, which represents the cognitive aspect of subjective well-being. The second would be obedience to divine orders and compliance with mandatory practices that, when performed, provide positive feelings and a sense of well-being for having fulfilled one's duty. And finally, the third requirement would be abstaining from sins and from everything that is prohibited by religion. By acting in this way, people reduce the chances of experiencing negative emotions that arise after committing an illicit act, such as guilt, regret, sadness, among others.

In their studies, authors like Amiruddin et al. (2021) also mention Islamic teachings that can contribute to happiness. The first of these is remembrance of God, with the aim of strengthening the spiritual connection and reducing excessive focus on worldly material pleasures. The second is trust in God (*tawakkul*), which strengthens hope and the process of resilience, providing security, stability, and reducing worry and anxiety about the future. The third would be adherence to values in order to promote spiritual growth and evolution, in addition to giving meaning to existence. The fourth teaching is satisfaction with life, which, according to the authors, would be one of the decisive elements for happiness because, if people do not have the ability to feel satisfied with what they have, they will probably also not feel lasting satisfaction when achieving other desired goals. The fifth element is hope, focusing on optimistic projections of the future. The sixth element is the clear and defined purpose that aims to direct human actions and give meaning to life. Believing in the existence of happiness is the seventh element, which, according to the authors, is essential to prevent the person from giving in to discouragement and helplessness.

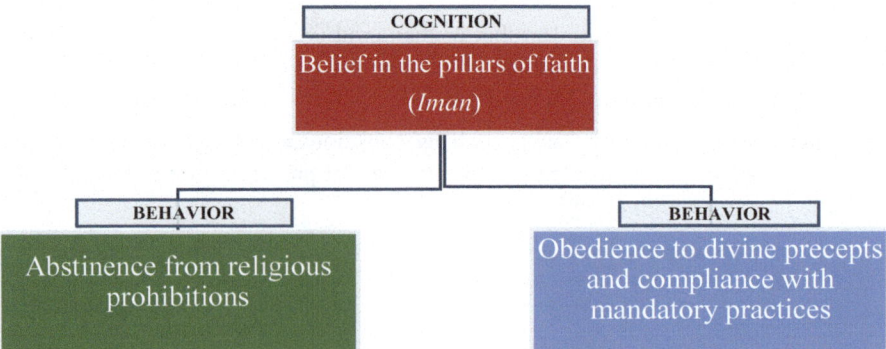

Fig. 5.6 Requirements for happiness according to Eryilmaz and Kula (2020)—Adapted by the author

The eighth element is to avoid excessive and unnecessary rituals, thus, precluding discomfort and overloading the person instead of balance. And finally, the ninth and tenth elements would be honesty, which provides peace of mind and respect, and optimism or positivity, with the objective of overcoming pessimism and any type of negative judgment.

Another study, carried out by Wiliasih et al. (2024, p. 150), points out seven paths for achieving happiness, according to the Quran: "seeking halal sustenance, being content, sincere, strengthening piety, being patient, grateful, and always remembering Allāh SWT." The authors explain that one of the ways in which happiness appears in the Quran is through the word *Al-Falah*, whose meaning refers to success which, from a spiritual perspective, is not material success but rather that which results from faith, effort, and the practice of good (Fig. 5.7).

Another study developed by Aycan (2024), based on the works of Al-Balkhi and Al-Birgivi, also identifies three necessary steps for achieving psychological well-being in Islam: knowledge, intention, and action. The first step includes knowledge about self-awareness; about vices; *virtues*; about worldly existence, human beings, and psychological disorders; and about Islamic belief and ethics (Fig. 5.8).

Regarding the second stage, she emphasizes the importance of combining sincere intention with a constant process of self-evaluation and introspection by individuals about their cognitions, emotions, and behaviors to avoid falling into certain vices. The action stage is nothing more than the result and externalization of the beliefs and intentions, and of individuals' consistent and intentional commitment to practice good actions, seeking both their personal evolution and well-being, as well as social well-being.

Understanding the Islamic view of psychological processes is fundamental for developing models and conceptions of well-being, like the influence of spiritual beliefs and practices on cognition, emotions, and behavior—the factors that favor a balance between the internal structures of the soul, how they relate to each other, and the triggers that drive certain behaviors in individuals, generating positive or negative sensations and feelings. In fact, many of the models proposed by authors writing about Islamic psychology to explain these processes are directly or indirectly related to the theme proposed in this book, since the harmonious balance of these internal structures will contribute directly to psychospiritual well-being. For this reason, understanding the internal structure and mechanisms that influence individuals' ways of thinking, feeling, and acting, from an Islamic perspective, is a

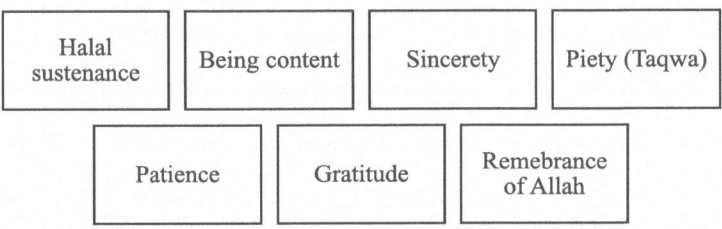

Fig. 5.7 Paths to happiness according to Wiliasih et al. (2024)—Adapted by the author

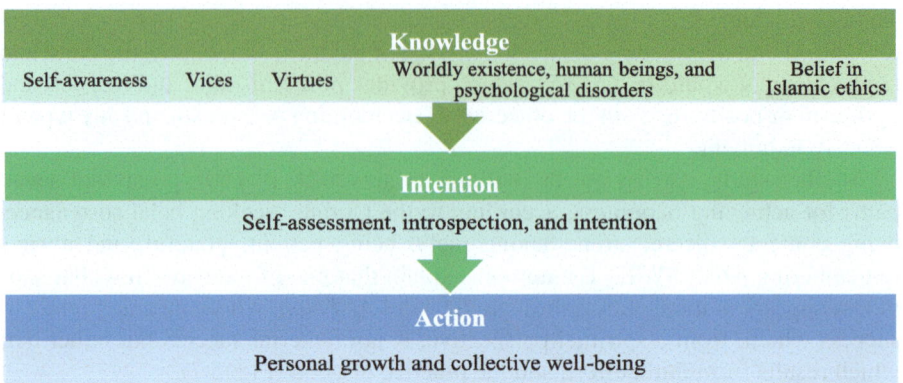

Fig. 5.8 Stages to psychological well-being based on the works of Al-Balkhi and Al-Birgivi according to Aycan (2024)—Adapted by the author

fundamental stage in the construction of hypotheses or specific conceptual models on well-being.

It is important to emphasize that the proposals presented throughout this chapter are not exhaustive, but a sample of models found in the literature. There are certainly limitations and gaps yet to be filled. The still reduced number of explanatory models, the often-exclusive focus on theoretical perspectives and hypotheses, as well as the scarcity of experimental research and the small number of samples examined in some studies, are among the limiting factors still persisting in the study of this theme. Most theoretical conceptions also disregard relevant factors like genetics and other biological aspects. Another also little-explored point is the reciprocal relationship between body and soul, that is, between psychospiritual factors and physical aspects, since both influence each other and are fundamental for well-being.

References

Al-Attas, S. M. N. (1995). *Prolegomena to the Metaphysics of Islam: An exposition of the Fundamental Elements of the Worldview of Islam*. Institute of Islamic Thought and Civilization (ISTAC).

Amiruddin, A., Qorib, M., & Zailani, Z. (2021). A study of the role of Islamic spirituality in happiness of Muslim citizens. *HTS Theological Studies, 77*(4), a6655. https://doi.org/10.4102/hts.v77i4.6655

Aycan, S. (2024). Construction of an Islamically-integrated psychological well-being model. *Journal of Muslim Mental Health, 18*(1), 46–61. https://doi.org/10.3998/jmmh.6026

Diener, E. (1984). Subjective well-being. *Psychological Bulletin, 95*(3), 542–575. https://doi.org/10.1037/0033-2909.95.3.542

Eryilmaz, A., & Kula, N. (2020). An investigation of Islamic well-being and mental health. *Journal of Religion and Health, 59*, 1096–1114. https://doi.org/10.1007/s10943-018-0588-0

Faruque, M. U. (2021). *Sculpting the self: Islam, selfhood and human flourishing*. University of Michigan Press.

Joshanloo, M. (2013). A comparison of western and Islamic conceptions of happiness. *Journal of Happiness Studies: An Interdisciplinary Forum on Subjective Well-Being, 14*(6), 1857–1874. https://doi.org/10.1007/s10902-012-9406-7

Joshanloo, M. (2017). Islamic conceptions of well-being. In R. Estes & M. Sirgy (Eds.), *The pursuit of human well-being. International Handbooks of Quality-of-Life*. Springer. https://doi.org/10.1007/978-3-319-39101-4_5

Joshanloo, M., & Weijers, D. (2019). Islamic perspectives on wellbeing. In L. Lambert & N. Pasha-Zaidi (Eds.), *Positive psychology in the Middle East/North Africa*. Springer. https://doi.org/10.1007/978-3-030-13921-6_11

Keshavarzi, H., & Ali, B. (2019). Islamic perspectives on psychological and spiritual well-being and treatment. In H. Moffic, J. Peteet, A. Hankir, & R. Awaad (Eds.), *Islamophobia and psychiatry* (pp. 41–53). Springer.

Keshavarzi, H., & Haque, A. (2013). Outlining a psychotherapy model for enhancing Muslim mental health within an Islamic context. *International Journal for the Psychology of Religion, 23*(3), 230–249. https://doi.org/10.1080/10508619.2012.712000

Keshavarzi, H., & Khan, F. (2018). Outlining a case illustration of Traditional Islamically Integrated Psychotherapy (TIIP). In C. Y. Al-Karam (Ed.), *Islamically integrated psychotherapy: Uniting faith and professional practice* (pp. 175–207). Templeton Press.

Keshavarzi, H., Keshavarzi, S. (2021). Emotionally oriented psychotherapy. In H. Keshavarzi, F. Khan, B. Ali, & R. Awaad (Eds.), *Applying Islamic Principles to Clinical Mental Health Care. Introducing Traditional Islamically Integrated Psychotherapy* (pp. 171–208). Routledge.

Keshavarzi, H., Khan, F., Ali, B., & Awaad, R. (2021). *Applying Islamic principles to clinical mental health care. Introducing Traditional Islamically Integrated Psychotherapy*. Routledge.

Khodayarifard, M., Ghobari-Bonab, B., Zardkhaneh, S. A., Zamanpour, E., & Derakhshan, M. (2016). Positive psychology from Islamic perspective. *International Journal of Behavioural Science, 10*, 77–83. http://www.behavsci.ir/article_67938_417fa8cefe57ac2a54443482 5a5c0551.pdf

Munsoor, M. S. (2021). *Wellbeing and the worshipper*. Springer.

Nasr, S. H. (2008). *Islamic spirituality*. Routledge.

Rothman, A., & Coyle, A. (2018). Toward a framework for Islamic psychology and psychotherapy: An Islamic model of the soul. *Journal of Religion and Health, 57*(5), 1731–1744. https://doi.org/10.1007/s10943-018-0651-x

Skinner, R. (2018). Traditions, paradigms and basic concepts in Islamic psychology. *Journal of Religion and Health, 58*(4), 1087–1094. https://doi.org/10.1007/s10943-018-0595-1

The Clear Quran. (n.d.). (M. Khattab, Trans.). https://Quran.com/

Wahab, M. A. (2022). Islamic spiritual and emotional intelligence and its relationship to eternal happiness: A conceptual paper. *Journal of Religion and Health, 61*(6), 4783–4806. https://doi.org/10.1007/s10943-021-01485-2

Wiliasih, R., Siregar, H., Irawan, T., & Beik, I. S. (2024). Happiness in Islam and influencing factors (SLR approach). *Al-Muzara'ah – Journal of Islamic Economics & Finance, 12*(1), 137–157. https://doi.org/10.29244/jam.12.1.137-157

Yusuf, A., & Elhadad, H. (2020). The use of the intellect ('Aql) as a cognitive restructuring tool in an Islamic psychotherapy. In H. Keshavarzi, F. Khan, B. Ali, & R. Awaad (Eds.), *Applying Islamic principles to clinical mental health care. Introducing Traditional Islamically Integrated Psychotherapy* (pp. 209–235). Routledge.

Chapter 6
The Islamic Model of Well-Being—A Holistic Perspective Derived from the Individual's Relationship with God, Self, and the Divine Creation

The harmonious integration of internal forces and structures based on faith and a virtuous life, as guided by the Quran, characterizes the holistic paradigm of well-being in Islam. The Islamic perspective of happiness and well-being depends on a state of harmony that integrates internal and external elements. Internal balance results from a harmonious relationship among the elements of the soul (heart, intellect, spirit, and the self). External balance would be the harmonious result of this internal dynamic of people with the external environment, harmony between the soul and the body, and between people and the surrounding environment. This is what makes individual and social well-being intertwined constructs (Fig. 6.1).

This concept reflects a eudaimonic concept of happiness. The feeling of satisfaction that represents well-being's highest level is achieved through internal balance among the soul's elements and external balance through a harmonious relationship among individuals in relation to God and individuals with society and the environment. This is a reciprocal relationship, since external stimuli have an impact on the internal state, just as internal dynamics have an impact on people's external actions.

In general, literature offers various models with elements that contribute to mental health and well-being. From a Western perspective, well-being is a broad and complex construct. Since it is a concept that involves quality of life and satisfaction with life, models that include all areas of life would be necessary, including genetic, cultural, socioeconomic, political, environmental, and other influences necessary to meet human needs. However, according to Joshanloo and Weijers (2019, p. 31), numerous authors have tried to explain well-being, but they realize that "such a complete understanding is beyond human capacity."

Although Islam encourages the pursuit of knowledge, if, given its magnitude, this is a science that humans still cannot attain, we can affirm that the orientations given by the One who created human beings and who fully knows their nature and needs could indicate the paths to achieve a true state of well-being. Hence, we find the importance of using religious teachings and their primary sources as a basis for unraveling this subject. For some, this difficulty in finding a "recipe" for well-being

S. Omais, *Happiness and Well-Being in Islam*,
https://doi.org/10.1007/978-3-031-95353-8_6

Fig. 6.1 Simplified model of well-being

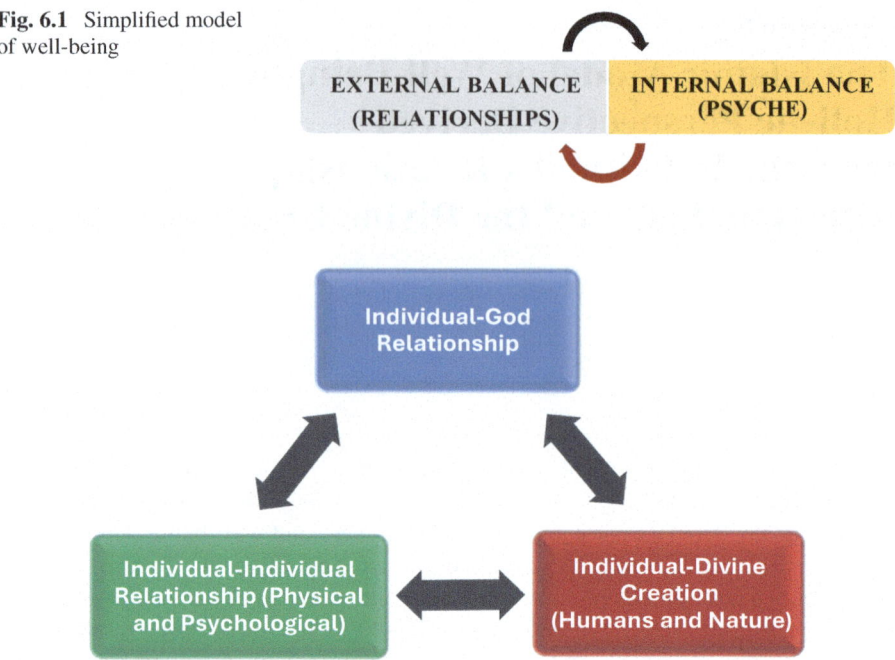

Fig. 6.2 The Islamic holistic model of well-being

is due to the very lack of real and lasting well-being on the earthly plane. It only occurs in the afterlife. Therefore, there is no way to uncover or "force" the existence of something that does not exist in this life or whose existence is incomplete. What exists in worldly life are moments of happiness or moments of well-being, and these, according to the literature, would only be possible through faith and alignment with religious and spiritual precepts (Joshanloo & Weijers, 2019).

By uniting all the knowledge cited throughout this text, it is possible to illustrate a conception that unites important elements for well-being in three spheres with which human beings interact: individuals with God, individuals with themselves, and individuals with their external environment, that is, their relationship with other beings, whether human or nonhuman (Fig. 6.2).

This model does not exhaust the countless variables we can link to well-being, but it does show the connection among the three main bases that stabilize this structure and the way in which this dynamic occurs. In reality, trying to include all possible variables that can influence well-being might be humanly impossible. However, if we use bases that represent at least the most essential dimensions for humans, such as spirituality, psychological and physical health, and the social/environmental context, we can have a more simplified and realistic perspective of well-being. We should also remember that the individual–divine creation present in this model encompasses social as well as political and economic aspects, and everything else that requires human interaction with the environment and God's creation. We should also emphasize that any and all divisions made here only serve as a didactic resource for studying them separately, because in practice, all these spheres are intimately connected, making it extremely difficult to separate them.

The model shown in Figs. 6.3 and 6.4 is a generic prototype of the Islamic perspective of well-being, which will be explained in detail in the following sections. The spiritual dimension is the starting point, the foundation that provides the coordinates for the balance between the individual (physical and psychological well-being) and the rest of the divine creation, including humans and nature. This is why it is represented in an overall relationship, to illustrate how these three dimensions are interconnected.

As a religion that is a lifestyle incorporated into all dimensions of an individual's life, Islam is a guide that includes directives for spiritual, physical, and emotional health, conduct, and prosocial behavior (*akhlaq* and *adab*). In order to simplify this model, we must emphasize that social well-being is a broad field that also encompasses the most diverse types of relationships—marital, family, professional, economic, political—and any other factors that affect collective well-being, such as the environment and the relationship with God's Creation. We must therefore make a few comments about the expression "Divine Creation." As it is a spiritual model based on Islamic teachings and faith, the idea that all beings with whom individuals relate are part of divine creation broadens the respect they are due and includes all relationships as necessary and essential dimensions for humans' holistic well-being. The following topics will explain in more detail each of the three dimensions of the Islamic *Triadic Model of Well-Being Based on Spiritually Interconnected Relationships*.

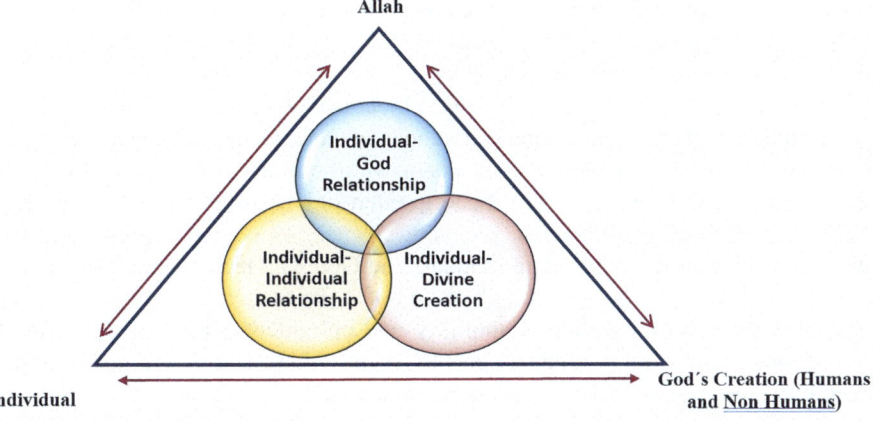

Fig. 6.3 The Islamic triadic model of well-being based on spiritually interconnected relationships (Elaborated by the Author)

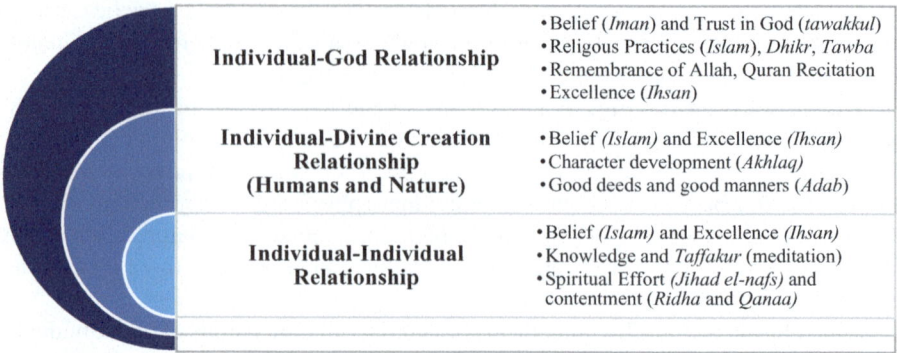

Individual-God Relationship	• Belief (*Iman*) and Trust in God (*tawakkul*) • Religous Practices (*Islam*), *Dhikr, Tawba* • Remembrance of Allah, Quran Recitation • Excellence (*Ihsan*)
Individual-Divine Creation Relationship (Humans and Nature)	• Belief *(Islam)* and Excellence *(Ihsan)* • Character development (*Akhlaq*) • Good deeds and good manners (*Adab*)
Individual-Individual Relationship	• Belief *(Islam)* and Excellence *(Ihsan)* • Knowledge and *Taffakur* (meditation) • Spiritual Effort *(Jihad el-nafs)* and contentment (*Ridha* and *Qanaa*)

Fig. 6.4 The dynamic of the Islamic triadic model of well-being based on spiritually interconnected relationships (Proposed by the Author)

6.1   The Individual–God Relationship

Muslims' religious and spiritual beliefs are a guide for every type of relationship they establish in their surroundings, from their relationship with God to their own thoughts, behaviors, and emotions. This includes their relationship with family, friends, co-workers, groups, and communities, as well as beliefs regulating and directing their behavior toward animals, nature, and creation in general.

The concept of health in Islam is not limited to the absence of physical or emotional illnesses but, above all, includes improvement of one's spiritual characteristics (Keshavarzi & Khan, 2018). A state of full health and physical, mental, or social well-being depends first and foremost on individuals' spiritual health. Joshanloo (2017) argues that, from the Quranic perspective, there is no well-being without faith and religion practiced both profoundly and habitually. The strength of life is in the essence of the soul, the spirit, and it is through the spirit that the soul connects to God. The spirit (*rūḥ*) represents the force of life, the divine breath, the spiritual component that connects individuals to God and guides the soul to higher stages, distancing it from its lower self and vices.

About the spirit (*rūḥ*) specifically, the subject is still an enigma. The Quran itself reveals that not all mysteries of the spirit can be unveiled by human beings, stressing that: "They will ask you about the spirit. Answer them: the spirit is one of the commands of my Lord, and you have been granted only a small part of knowledge" (Quran 17:85, interpretation of the meaning). Hence, we see the importance of nurturing this relationship between individuals and God with practices that nourish and educate the spirit, and not just the physical body, the matter. The Quran states that remembrance of God provides tranquility and enlightens humans' hearts, unlike that of those who do not connect spiritually and whose hearts end up hardening, since it is there that spiritual light shines and spreads.

From the Islamic perspective, people's level of satisfaction and well-being results more from their awareness and the cognitive-spiritual balance they make of their behavior than from feelings and emotions themselves. An illicit act (*haram*) that initially generates pleasure and joy can turn into a negative emotion when people become aware of its prohibited nature. In this case, the positive emotion fades as soon as people become aware of the mismatch between their act and spiritual teachings. Islamic spiritual teachings aim not only to protect individual and collective well-being. The spiritual well-being that arises from conformity to divine precepts both protects individuals from the insatiable urges of their desires and prevents the formation of an individualistic society focused only on individual satisfaction and well-being.

Moments of well-being provided in worldly life are directly linked to faith and obedience to divine precepts because it is from these that individuals can feel a state of tranquility and peace of mind. The soul's four elements are necessary to establish individuals' relationship with God, and faith provides the guidelines to help Muslims balance impulses and desires that often generate pain and unhappiness. Without strong faith, it is difficult to achieve psychological or social well-being, since it is faith that gives meaning to human existence and provides more lasting positive experiences, unlike the quick and fleeting pleasures that characterize hedonia. Suffering, pain, and life's challenges need a firm foundation so that they can be circumvented and overcome. Religion provides meanings that help cognitively reinterpret such situations in a positive and hopeful way, as opportunities for growth and to be rewarded for the difficulties faced. Such resources can provide reassurance and security (Joshanloo, 2017).

The individual–God relationship includes not only faith in the abstract sense but also practices that strengthen the spirit and promote a balance between the material and spiritual worlds. In order for this internal relationship to be established in harmony, we must first understand how it happens. The balance between the soul's inner forces (*aql, ruh, nafs*, and *qalb*), aligned with religious guidelines generates a state of consciousness and inner peace that results in individual well-being. This is one of the keys to a good life capable of providing tranquility and contentment. Thus, for example, in order for the spirit (*rūḥ*) to be strengthened through the practices of *dhikr*, prayer, or reading the Quran, it needs an intellect (*aql*) that first absorbs and understands the principles of faith, the basis that will serve as motivation for all other actions. Understanding the pillars of faith through the intellect and reasoning strengthens the spirit. This, in turn, compels people to practice important spiritual acts such as contemplation (*taffakur*) and *muraqabat*, as well as memorizing, reciting, understanding, and reflecting on the teachings of the Quran and the *Sunnah*. It is through the *aql* that people will establish the foundation of belief, based on the six pillars of faith, trust in God (*tawakkul*), and also the ethical-moral and legal teachings (*shariah*), which will be decisive for developing character and directing the behavior and inclinations of the *nafs*. This *nafs*, in turn, stimulated by this more intimate connection with God, leads individuals to charitable deeds and spiritual practices.

We must point out that faith is an element that needs to be nourished both through knowledge and through actions and behavior. *Iman* is the energy that provides security, certainty, and strength for individuals to maintain their religious purpose. At the same time, it is also related to various psychic functions, such as cognition, emotion, and motivation, as well as to well-being, as it aligns with the human being's *fitrah*, providing tranquility for the soul (Utz, 2011). The absence of *Iman* can lead to empty people lacking sufficient motivation to persist in their goals. Righteous behavior has repercussions on the relationship between individuals and God, as it brings them closer to their *fitrah*, their pure nature, strengthening their connection with God.

Many practical examples serve to strengthen this connection between God and individuals. We must emphasize that all permissible behavior in Islam is considered a spiritual act or act of worship, which Utz (2011) divides into actions linked to the heart, tongue, body, belief, and wealth. Among spiritual actions linked to the heart, the author cites love, hope, submission, repentance, trust, and fear of God, among others. Actions linked to the tongue include supplication, remembrance, and recitation of the Quran. Physical actions would be traditional rites such as prayer, fasting, and Hajj, while financial actions would be charity and other donations (Utz, 2011).

By invigorating the spirit (*rūḥ*), spiritual practices also reverberate positively in the heart, enlightening it and generating a feeling of tranquility, peace, and contentment (*ridha*). Considering that emotions are directly linked to the heart, and that a person's emotional state reverberates through all the body's organs and their physical health, we can see how the Individual–God relationship is broad and extremely relevant to well-being. This relationship is the primary basis for the other relationships individuals establish, either with themselves or with the environment around them.

6.2   The Individual–Individual Relationship

The dynamic understanding among the elements of the soul referred to in the Quran as the heart (*qalb*), the inclinations of the soul (*nafs*), the intellect (*aql*), and the spirit (*rūḥ*) is fundamental to understanding the idea of psychospiritual well-being in Islam. As explained in the previous chapter, unlike the Western view, in Islamic psychology, the term "soul" refers not only to the spiritual aspect but also to a set of all psychological functions (cognitions, emotions, behaviors) and spiritual functions interacting with each other simultaneously (Keshavarzi et al., 2021).

The term *nafs* in the Quran refers to both the sense of self/ego and the sense of soul. It is the element that represents humans' immaterial structure, all people's essence that includes the self, the ego, the personality, and their behavioral inclinations. The *nafs* can sometimes be more inclined toward primitive impulses, passions, and desires, when individuals disconnect from God and surrender to their lower nature. The intellect (*aql*), in turn, represents reason, the ability to discern good and evil, right and wrong. It is the intellect that guides people based on their knowledge of the world, creation, and God (Keshavarzi et al., 2021; Munsoor, 2021; Rothman & Coyle, 2018).

Human life is not something passive, where situations arise without people having any responsibility for them. It is not life's circumstances that determine people's emotional state, but rather the way in which they react to them, and also how they take responsibility for their actions. Free will, responsibility, and decision-making are determining factors for well-being, since they define how individuals will act, the consequences of their conduct, and their commitment to the process of evolution and improvement. The Quran confirms this when it states that "Indeed, Allah does not wrong people in the least, but it is people who wrong themselves" (Quran, 10:44) and also by the verse that states, "Indeed, Allah would never change a people's state until they change their own state" (Quran, 13:11, interpretation of the meaning). These verses reaffirm all people's responsibility for their actions and, above all, for their own process of change. Cognition is one of the central elements influencing the decision-making process that directs human behavior. This is why we must discuss some points that connect it to individuals' well-being.

6.2.1 Psychospiritual Well-Being as a Result of Cognition

Decisions made by individuals can generally be guided by a rational process based on more elaborate beliefs and cognitions, or by impulses and desires, based on human beings' instinctive nature. Human beings make countless decisions every day, and their emotional state is linked to both the quality of their choices and their actions, as well as the way in which they interpret the events that happen to them. Decisions are formed based on beliefs and values that are most relevant to them. Individuals who learn throughout life that happiness should be enjoyed to the fullest will probably make decisions that can provide them with important levels of pleasure, maintaining a constant search for this goal, which can sometimes be obsessive and frustrating. It is clear that this requires a paradigm shift and a process of reframing and cognitive reconstruction of more realistic concepts of happiness. A concept that is learned incorrectly and is far removed from reality can create unrealistic expectations, leading subjects to dysfunctional behavior. On the other hand, people who understand that there is no lasting happiness in worldly life, in the material world, will have to change their focus and exchange the unbridled search for external goals for a search within themselves, in internal and more abstract resources such as faith, spirituality, love, peace, hope, wisdom, and satisfaction, among others. By guiding themselves using these values, people begin to invest in a happiness that not only serves their desires, but other dimensions that go beyond themselves.

One of the first steps to promoting psychological well-being at an individual level is to start with cognition and the way the subject interprets the world and life events. The inclusion of positive and optimistic thoughts to counter negative thoughts of the *aql* is one of the strategies also widely encouraged in Islam (Rothman, 2018). Therefore, as the literature mentions, there is an intermingling between the objective dimension, represented by religious guidance and submission to religious prescriptions, and the subjective dimension that results from the self's harmony with that guidance.

The incorporation of Islamic teachings and precepts takes place at the level of the intellect (*aql*) through learning, understanding, and reasoning that strengthen the spiritual dimension (*rūḥ*) via knowledge and help solidify character (*akhlaq*). This process assists in consolidating the motivations that will serve as the basis for the *aql*'s decision-making to balance the *nafs*' desires and impulses. An intellect (*aql*) with little spiritual knowledge, combined with a spirit (*rūḥ*) weakened by a lack of spiritual practices, is overcome by the *nafs al ammarah*'s desires. If this occurs, the critical self (*nafs al lawammah*), represented by the conscience and formed by the union of the *aql*, *rūḥ*, and *nafs*, activates emotional states of guilt, sadness, restlessness, anguish, and regret in the *qalb*, which have negative repercussions on the physical and psychological spheres. Therefore, the God–individual relationship precedes the other relationships in the *Islamic Triadic Model*, since it is the relationship that will guide them.

We can thus see that, from a psychological point of view, individual well-being revolves entirely around these internal elements. This does not diminish the importance of biological and genetic factors, as well as external factors related to the environment. However, the harmony among the soul's inner forces is decisive in overcoming some of these factors. This explains, for example, why people living in poverty and having a scarcity of material resources are able to share what little they have with their peers, while many financially well-off individuals are not generous and are afraid of losing their wealth if they share it with others. Scenes, for example, from the genocide in Gaza, spread on social media, show Palestinian refugees experiencing extreme food scarcity sharing their food not only with their peers but also giving up their food to share with cats and other animals. This reality completely contradicts some classic theories of psychology, such as Abraham Maslow's hierarchy of needs, which conjectured that an individual who did not meet their biological needs would be unable to reach the highest stage of self-actualization. The scenario during the genocide shows people who, even though their physiological or safety needs are not met, represent the higher levels of Maslow's pyramid. That is, they forgo their own satisfaction to satisfy others.

This is just one example of countless situations in which spirituality and character (*akhlaq*) overcome the self's desires and impulses, leading it to more supportive and spiritually elevated attitudes, even when the context is extremely adverse. Thus, the concept of individual well-being in Islam needs to be understood from a psychospiritual point of view, not just from a psychic one. Although Maslow's theory of needs makes some sense, it focuses on individual desires and needs, under the logic that individuals must first meet their own needs before they can contribute socially or evolve morally and spiritually. In addition to being an individualistic perspective, the theory assumes that spiritual evolution is only possible after the satisfaction of physical-biological needs, while in Islam, spiritual evolution is the primary basis that sustains and directs all other human needs and behaviors. Perhaps it is no wonder that Maslow recognized at the end of his life that he should have given greater focus to the study of spirituality in his theory.

6.2.2 Psychospiritual Well-Being as a Result of Positive Emotions

If we talk about well-being, we must also talk about emotions. Based on several current references, we have explained throughout this book how this state of peace and tranquility (*nafs al-mutmainah*) is achieved spiritually, in abstract terms, through the effort of the soul. From a practical point of view, this state of *sakinah* (tranquility) perceived internally results from both behaviors and cognition. Emotions do not arise from nowhere; they need some stimulus, whether internal or external. Focusing only on emotions would be the same as treating a symptom without addressing the problem's cause. If positive emotions are responses to a person's evaluation and interpretation of circumstances, then they depend first and foremost on a cognitive process that emits signals so that these responses are positive. These signals are the subjective interpretations, the meanings that each person attributes to events. Emotions are triggered by cognition, and therefore, we cannot talk about positive emotions without first giving due attention to the positive cognitions that give rise to them, that is, to the meanings given to events. In this context, religious values, beliefs, and content stand out as fundamental elements in this process.

A systematic review conducted by Wiliasih et al. (2024) in Indonesia on the factors influencing happiness in Islam found that peace and tranquility are the truest and highest forms of happiness, and such feelings result from the person's closeness to God. As mentioned before, the satisfaction of immediate and unlimited pleasure is not the true source of happiness, much less moments of euphoria and ecstasy. It is, rather, a light and peaceful conscience, capable of adapting one's behavior to the limits established by one's beliefs, principles, and values that are higher than human desires. Therefore, one of the ways to achieve this state of contentment occurs when, after an internal conflict, the critical self manages to stand out from the self of desires and overcome this dispute. This results in a tranquility of conscience due to not infringing moral and/or religious values and principles. It also, in the end, contributes to the sense of self-efficacy as people realize their ability to dominate their desires instead of being dominated by them. Thus, the spiritual concept of happiness' most characteristic positive affect in Islam is not represented by euphoric states or highly excitable emotions, but rather by gentle sensations such as calm, satisfaction, and serenity.

6.2.2.1 Cognitions, Emotions, Behaviors, and Resilience from an Islamic Perspective

Emotions and cognitions are closely related to well-being and are fundamental to the process of resilience. Life satisfaction and well-being are related to both positive emotions and cognitive skills like problem-solving, resignification, and emotional regulation (Cohn et al., 2009). Cognition helps to re-signify adverse situations and create new alternatives. Positive emotions expand cognition and the possibilities of thought-action through the construction of more lasting personal resources. By expanding thinking, it also expands the repertoire for problem-solving and facing adverse situations. This allows for strengthening resilience and improving well-being over time (Fredrickson, 2001).

There is a reciprocal movement among cognition, emotions, and behaviors, any of which can be the initial trigger of the psychic process. In the behavioral aspect, after being practiced by the individual, actions are evaluated by consciousness, by perception, that is, by a general cognitive evaluation that indicates whether that act or attitude was good or bad, right, or wrong. Likewise, in the cognitive aspect, optimistic and hopeful perspectives generate emotions of enthusiasm that direct behavior positively. Emotions can also be this process's initial trigger, whether positive or negative, as both can give impetus to virtuous behaviors. Negative emotions linked to spirituality, such as the fear of God, influence the cognitive process of decision-making, which will in turn drive people to do something good or stop doing something bad.

Religious beliefs offer answers to existential anxieties and concerns such as death or the meaning of life. This relationship generates more adaptive patterns of emotional regulation, self-efficacy, and increased controllability of emotions. Resources such as acceptance and cognitive reassessment also have an intrinsic relationship with religiosity, providing a higher frequency of positive rather than negative emotional experiences (Vishkin et al., 2019). Positive emotions can be the result of cognition derived from religious beliefs, as well as from behaviors related to rites and virtuous conduct. The union of cognition, emotions, and positive behaviors involved with R/S creates a cycle that feeds back on itself (Fig. 6.5).

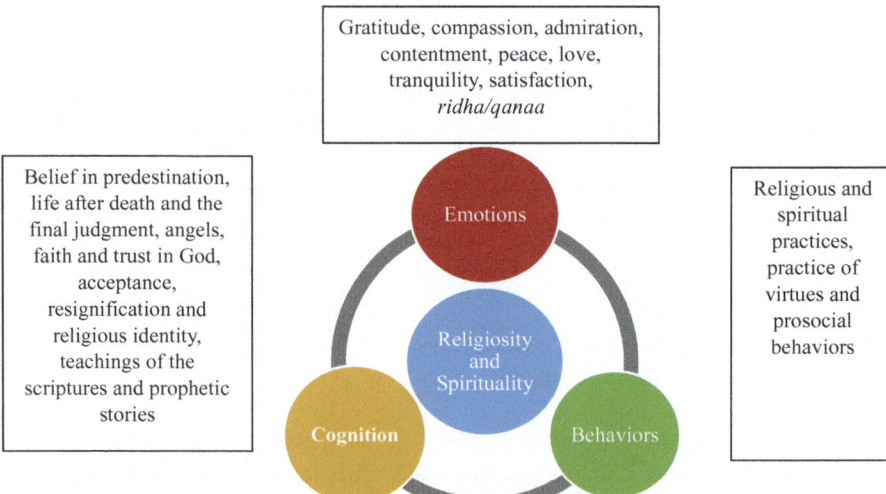

Fig. 6.5 Cognition–emotion–behavior cycle from an Islamic spiritual perspective (Elaborated by the Author)

Religious cognition plays a fundamental role in positively influencing emotions. In the cognitive aspect, belief in the pillars of faith is essential to provide calm, relief, confidence, hope, and optimism, which in turn will encourage individuals to persist in their actions and achieve new achievements. We should note that accomplishment is one of the pillars of well-being and a stage of the psychospiritual process that unfolds internally until it is externalized through actions. Belief and trust in God (*tawakkul*), as well as belief in the existence of angels, in sacred scriptures, in prophets and their life stories, in predestination, and in the Last Judgment, are cognitions that influence individuals' decisions and behaviors, the interpretations of life events, and, consequently, their emotional state. This is the influence of cognition on the person's emotions.

It is also important to draw attention to other emotional states related to satisfaction and contentment (*ridha and qanaa*). Satisfaction with what an individual has is an element that reduces feelings of hopelessness and anxiety (Wiliasih et al., 2024), and the relationship of this concept to well-being makes it essential to delve deeper into this topic, which we discuss below.

6.2.3 **Ridha***: An Important Resource for Psychospiritual Well-Being and Resilience*

Ridha is, at the same time, an attitude and a feeling that combines acceptance and satisfaction. It is an attitude of nonopposition and calm, which generates greater psychological flexibility in the face of life's events. The difference is that this satisfaction does not depend solely on an individual's emotional state, but above all on a spiritual understanding associated with God, which gives it a more positive meaning than acceptance. *Qanaa*, on the other hand, is one of the initial stages of *ridha*, when individuals are already convinced of the situation (Khalil, 2014). In the case of *ridha*, there is a process of acceptance that involves spiritual beliefs, such as trust in divine designs, for example. Belief in predestination is another important example of satisfaction, as in *ridha* the individual not only stops opposing the event but also seeks to feel satisfied (Sholichatun, 2023).

Ibn Al-Qayim al Jawziyya (2020) explains that there are various levels of *ridha*, from the most basic, such as satisfaction with all divine commands, actions, prescriptions, and decrees, to the highest level, which is represented by love, fear, trust, and gratitude to God. For Ibn Al-Qayim (2020), gratitude is at a higher level than satisfaction, and the path that leads individuals to it is precisely *ridha* (Al-Qarni, 2005). Being grateful for good things has a certain logic, while being grateful for bad things not make much sense. However, in Islam, gratitude is not a practice directed only toward good times or good things, but also toward bad times, since many situations are not always understandable to humans, according to this Quranic quote: "Perhaps you dislike something which is good for you and like something which is bad for you. Allah Knows and you do not know" (2:216). Prophet Muhammad (ﷺ) also reinforced this, saying: "'From (the signs of) the son of Adam's prosperity, is his satisfaction with what Allah decreed for him" (Tirmidhî) and also "be satisfied with what Allah has alloted for you and you shall be the richest of the people" (At-Tirmidhi). There is another Hadīth that states:

> How wonderful is the case of a believer; there is good for him in everything and this applies only to a believer. If prosperity attends him, he expresses gratitude to Allah and that is good for him; and if adversity befalls him, he endures it patiently and that is better for him (Muslim)

The most significant difference between satisfaction from an Islamic perspective and satisfaction and/or gratitude from a Western perspective is that in Islam, *ridha* encompasses both satisfaction with good things and bad things, while in the secular view, the focus of gratitude tends to be only on good things. This satisfaction is not with the negative situation itself, nor is it a way of denying reality, but rather of feeling satisfied with divine designs, because in addition to accepting, the person also trusts and believes that there is always something beneficial in divine designs, and thus avoids a defensive or rebellious reaction. Contrary to *ridha*, nonacceptance and dissatisfaction encourage mental rumination, worry, negative thoughts about oneself and God, anger, complaints, bitterness, impatience, doubts, resentment, restlessness, anguish, and anxiety, all feelings that oppose well-being. The refusal to accept facts, together with resentment and dissatisfaction, ends up prolonging pain and suffering's duration, delaying the process of coping. On the other hand, satisfaction promotes a feeling of lightness by alleviating the cognitive and emotional burden that many carry due to an exhaustive search for logical explanations and the blaming of themselves and others (Al-Qarni, 2005; Sholichatun, 2023).

Ridha is, in fact, an important cognitive strategy to be used in interventions aimed at reframing negative situations and emotions experienced by individuals. Satisfaction and acceptance of divine designs actually generate freedom—freedom from guilt, control, and the anguish of not understanding the reasons for certain events (Al-Qarni, 2005). This state of trust in God and destiny has an impact on the emotional state, contributing to a sense of well-being. According to Sholichatun (2023), *ridha* provides benefits in the cognitive, emotional, behavioral, and spiritual spheres, dimensions that are, in fact, linked to each other. In the cognitive sphere, *ridha* is constructed based on religious meanings and explanations that contribute to coping with the situation, such as trust in God and the divine plan. Thus, the Islamic view's conception of *ridha* can have a positive effect both in relation to the blessings and benefits that arise in good times and in the process of resilience in the face of bad times. In the Islamic perspective, the latter can also have many benefits that are not always perceived immediately. These include deliverance from something worse, or the expectation of being rewarded in the future for suffering, or even the possibility of such vicissitudes strengthening or generating an internal transformation in the individual.

Ridha is an element fused with faith, and therefore, this satisfaction is related to belief in God and His laws, resulting in a state of calm, peace of mind, and tranquility that gradually restores strength and resilience to face the situation. Satisfaction and contentment also generate a sense of comfort and security (Al-Qarni, 2005). Hence, the behavioral benefits arise from *ridha*, given that emotional unblocking broadens the vision and problem-solving capacity, taking the person out of the state of paralysis and inaction. In simple terms, satisfaction is a way to eliminate worry, the search for answers, and ruminative thinking. By removing these elements that usually paralyze individuals, the process of overcoming becomes faster. If we make an analogy with Fredrickson's broaden-and-build theory (2009), where positive emotions have an effect that expands cognitive functions and drives action while negative emotions reduce cognitive functions and narrow the spectrum of action, we can see that *ridha* is a positive strategy.

In the Quran (5:119), *ridha* is usually expressed as a feeling of reciprocity between the human soul and God, from one to the other. Therefore, according to Khalil (2014), there are authors who define it as a state of satisfaction between God and the human soul. It is an elevated level of spirituality that also provides peace, which, according to Khalil (2014, p. 375), results from the "surrendering of the heart to God's eternal decree, from abdicating the impulse to control one's destiny. Such a renunciation of will produces a sense of tranquility infinitely greater than any experience of discomfort or pain which may follow as a consequence of the unpredictable and shifting sands of fate." The author also adds that *ridha* is a humble recognition of the human intellect "that, in His omniscience, God has in mind the best interests of the soul" (Khalil, 2014, p. 376). And this is only possible if there is a relationship of deep and unshakable trust, the trust of faith.

Relativization in the interpretation of adversities taught in Islam contributes to the balance between positive and negative emotions and to emotional stability, as opposed to indignation, rebellion, and denial. And to achieve emotional stability, there must also be spiritual stability, where the relationship with the divine is not conditioned only by good things but remains firm when the individual is afflicted by evil. Positive emotions are as central to well-being as the heart (*qalb*) is central to all physical and psychological functioning. This emotional balance or imbalance has repercussions on the body and ends up being projected onto the external environment in the form of actions.

6.2.4 Psychospiritual Well-Being as a Result of Religious, Ethical, and Moral Behavior (Akhlaq and Adab)

Human behavior can have a positive or negative impact on emotions. We can divide the behavioral element into two categories: behaviors related to religious rituals and practices (individual–God), and the person's behavior in the social environment (individual–society) or with other creatures. This separation is actually for educational purposes only, since, as mentioned before, in Islam both religious rituals and everyday behavior are considered acts of worship (*ibadah*). Cappellen et al. (2023)

point out that positive emotions often emerge from spiritual or religious practices and postures (Cappellen et al., 2024), promoting a sense of well-being that encourages the repetition of these rituals, as well as pro-social behaviors. Therefore, rituals also mix directly or indirectly with social acts, such as prayers, charity, and pilgrimage. This logic explains why all Muslim behavior is linked to both God and the social environment at the same time.

Keshavarzi and Nsour (2021) state that the effort to change inappropriate behaviors into positive behaviors directly contributes to individuals' balance and holistic health. The behavioral aspect, which involves *adab, akhlaq*, and the practice of good deeds, can have positive repercussions on people's emotional state as they reduce the conflicts of the *nafs* with the soul's structures such as conscience, intellect (*aql*), spirit (*rūḥ*), and heart (*qalb*). The practice of virtues has already been widely reported in the literature of positive psychology as a great source of generating positive emotions, which is why it is also used in therapeutic interventions today (Rashid & Seligman, 2019).

From an Islamic perspective, the harmonious connection among the elements of the soul, spiritual practices, and the practice of virtues would be the path to evolution and to achieving an emotional state of comfort, peace, and tranquility. Therefore, practices and interventions that encourage individuals to increase these behaviors can contribute to emotional well-being. This state of happiness of the heart, fueled by belief and religious/spiritual practice, reverberates over Muslims' happiness. The union between belief and the practice of virtues aligns with the Quranic verse that says: "Whoever does good, whether man or woman, and is a believer, We will grant a pleasant life, and We will reward him with a reward according to the best of deeds" (16:97).

The way to strengthen the spirit (*rūḥ*), purify the heart, and connect more with God is through acts of worship (*ibadah*). Although there are diverse levels, reading and reciting the Quran is an act of worship, just like a prayer, a *duaa, dhikr*, charity, an act of kindness, a kind word, and even a smile.

Moral behavior is connected to worship in Islam, and it involves everyday acts, whether small or large. Islam teaches that every action a human performs that is permitted by the religion (*halal*) is considered a good deed because it shows that the individual is making choices and behaving in accordance with what pleases Allah, as explained in the following Ḥadīth:

> In every ascription of glory to God, every declaration of His greatness, every utterance of praise to Him, every declaration that He is the only God, in enjoining what is reputable, in forbidding what is objectionable, and in a man's sexual intercourse there is *sadaqa*." On being asked whether a reward would be given for satisfying one's passion, he said, "Tell me; if he were to devote it to something forbidden, would it not be a sin on his part? Similarly, if he were to devote it to something lawful, he would have a reward." (Muslim)

6.2.4.1 Positive Emotions as a Result of Religious Practices and Rituals

The practice of religious rituals like prayer, fasting, charity, pilgrimage, recitation/ understanding of the Quran, and remembrance of God (*dhikr*) are behaviors that can contribute to this state of *sakinah*, through spirituality and by strengthening individuals' connection with God. There is no shortage of studies demonstrating the effects of Islamic spiritual practices, whether they relate to fasting, prayer, charity, pilgrimage, *dhikr*, or simply listening to the Quran. Both virtuous and religious behaviors are shown in Fig. 6.6.

Islamic Practices and Interventions for Promoting Psychospiritual Well-Being
The Quran emphasizes that whoever forgets Allah will, in fact, be forgetting his or her own soul. This forgetfulness of self becomes visible when people find themselves trapped in the "lower" self, leading them to focus on the satisfaction of physical desires and to distance themselves from their rational faculties and their own evolution as a person. The values constructed from religious and spiritual teachings broaden the spectrum of happiness from a material and individualistic focus to a spiritual happiness that transcends the person's world and expands to broader and more collective dimensions.

The struggle of the soul (*jihad el-nafs*) is considered the greatest and most challenging struggle that individuals face throughout their lives. It is a daily and continuous process involving choices that are often contrary to one's own self and against one's own will (Joshanloo & Weijers, 2019). Various daily situations in Muslims' lives activate this battle between the self of desires and the self-critical self. Therefore, from an Islamic perspective, will and desire do not guide people to happiness, but rather reason and the alignment of actions with spiritual guidance do. According to Munsoor (2021), the soul is like a fortress, and character, as well as conduct, would be the doors protecting it. Thus, a strong spiritual connection with

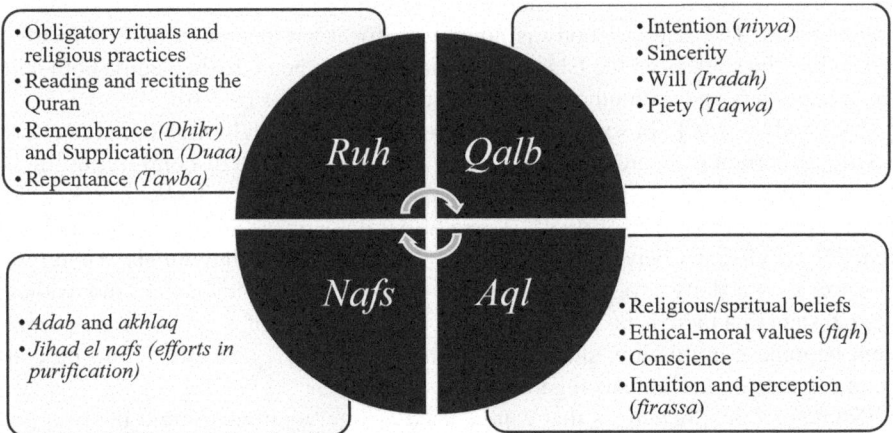

Fig. 6.6 Practices for the purification of the soul (*Tazkiyat El-Nafs*)—Adapted by the Author

the divine, together with the knowledge and absorption of ethical-religious principles, can facilitate the management of the self's desires and impulses.

Purification of the soul, through the improvement of character and conduct, gradually leads individuals to higher stages of consciousness that strengthen their relationship with God. The objective of this purification is to lead Muslims to the highest spiritual stage, providing people with relief and peace of mind (Alias & Samsudin, 2005). The processes of soul purification (*tazkiyat al nafs*) or training (*riyadat el nafs*) aim to discipline, educate and train the individual in self-control, and purify the heart so that it can remain connected with the divine.

Human beings have inclinations toward both good and evil. The more people are involved with worldly life and the material world, the more individuals distance themselves from the spiritual world, becoming more prone to selfishness and individualism than to the pursuit of the common good. On the other hand, faith and spirituality help occupy individuals' intellect, preventing them from descending to the lowest levels of human nature. One of the essential virtues for persisting in this process of purification and training the soul is patience (Joshanloo & Weijers, 2019).

According to Munsoor (2021), by surrendering to the *nafs'* lower and impulsive nature, humans would enter a downward spiral that culminates in the spiritual self's death. When analyzed through the lens of positive psychology, the negative impact of this becomes clear. Fredrickson's (2013) Broaden-and-Build Theory explains that positive emotions generate an upward spiral of well-being, creating a reinforcing cycle of positive experiences and behaviors. Conversely, negative thoughts and experiences mutually reinforce each other in a self-perpetuating cycle, deteriorating an individual's emotional and mental state and leading to a downward spiral. From an islamic perspective, a similar logic applies: spiritual disconnection weakens the individual's ability to tame the lower self, while the act itself further diminishes spiritual connection, negatively affecting one's cognitions, emotions, and behaviors. An individual's connection with their Creator is a process that must be constantly nourished, just as the body needs to be nourished with food so that it does not weaken or easily become ill. There is a visible similarity between the body's and the soul's needs. The physical body is nourished, for many people, with 3–5 meals a day, while the soul, from the Islamic perspective, must be nourished daily, both with the five prayers and with other complementary practices (Fig. 6.6).

The body needs to be exercised to become stronger, which often requires effort, giving up certain pleasures, and generating physical pain and discomfort until individuals adapt. The soul, when exercised, must also give up certain pleasures in order to strengthen and evolve spiritually. It needs to train patience and constancy until the practice of virtuous behaviors becomes a natural habit in individuals. Therefore, because it is a daily process that extends until life's end, Joshanloo and Weijers (2019) state that there is no possibility of achieving a state of well-being and permanent happiness in this life, since the very nature of life is unstable, requiring constant effort from individuals regarding their behavior.

Some practical resources that can be used as interventions to train the soul and improve individual well-being are repentance, supplication, self-awareness, contemplation, and remembrance of God. The latter can be accomplished through prayers, *dhikr*, as well as reading, understanding, and reciting the Quran. Besides these resources, there are some virtues that also contribute to spiritual evolution, according to Al-Attas (1995). He explains that there are virtues of a higher level, which make people turn to God, such as repentance (*tawbah*), patience (*sabr*), gratitude (*shukr*), hope (*raja*), fear (*khawf*), divine unity (*tawhid*), trust (*tawakkul*), and the greatest of them, divine love (*mahabbah*), the main path to happiness. The word repentance (*tawbah*) is mentioned 36 times in the Quran, and terms related to it, such as compassion and mercy, are divine attributes that appear at the beginning of each Quranic surah in the expression of *basmala*. Therefore, repentance is considered a spiritual practice encouraged in Islam, requiring humility and recognition of human beings' mistakes and imperfections (Rothman, 2018).

We can use interventions with Muslim patients that combine intellectual, spiritual, and behavioral aspects to increase levels of well-being. There is, for example, a notable focus on self-knowledge and self-reflection in Islam. By recognizing one's personal qualities and defects, the human being's rational side becomes more alert to the animal self's impulses (*nafs al amarah*). This state of alertness and self-awareness (*muraqabah*), in turn, provokes a state of self-reflection and self-criticism in individuals, prompting them to evaluate their own actions (*muhassabah*). Several verses of the Quran also encourage contemplation and reflection on divine creation, human nature, and the psychology of the soul, encouraging humans to expand their knowledge of themselves and the world around them.

Meditation, contemplation, and self-reflection enhance spiritual and personal evolution together along with the improvement in the practice of virtues. Contemplation (*taffakur*) is the Islamic practice of reflecting on divine attributes and creation, while meditation combines knowledge about God, nature, and self-reflection. Al-Ghazali mentions six stages for spiritual struggle (*jihad el nafs*) and purification of the soul. These are practices that expand individuals' awareness of their actions. The first of these, *musharata*, aims to raise awareness of triggers and everything that leads individuals to lose control and move away from spirituality. The second, *muraqaba*, is characterized by a state of attention and self-surveillance where individuals begin to monitor their own actions and the intentions behind them, a moment of introspection that makes them reflect internally about themselves and their relationships with others and with God. The third stage, *muhasaba*, is individuals' self-accountability, the self-critical side linked to *nafs al lawamah*. The fourth stage, *mu'aqaba*, is a preventive way of making a mistake by abstaining or refraining from a certain behavior or by rewarding oneself for successes and positive changes. *Mua'bata* is the fifth stage; its purpose is self-reproach or censure for bad behavior. However, this censure must not be excessive to the point of causing individuals harm due to excessive feelings of guilt or shame. This last stage, if carried out well, prevents individuals from normalizing such behaviors over time, preparing them to become aware of these actions in advance so that they do not happen again. And finally, the sixth stage, *mujahada*, is when people propose to try and try again to avoid bad behavior, seeking paths and environments that help curb these attitudes (Keshavarzi & Nsour, 2021; Munsoor, 2021).

6.2.5   Islamic Practices and Teachings That Encourage Self-Care and Individual Well-Being

Although the Islamic paradigm emphasizes collective well-being and the spiritual aspect, it does not ignore happiness and some individual goals. Various religious teachings encourage self-care and the satisfaction of human needs. Although subjective well-being plays a secondary role and sometimes takes second place to social well-being, it has its importance in Islam and comes from the combination of a virtuous life and a continuous connection with God (Joshanloo & Weijers, 2019). Islamic precepts themselves aim to protect individuals by ensuring that their needs, as well as those of society, are met.

Nevertheless, the Islamic religion does not occupy only the spiritual sphere of a Muslim's life and does not encourage asceticism. It covers all aspects of life, aiming at a complete integration with the individual so that the body's, soul's, and spirit's needs are satisfied. There are some *Hādīth* that confirm this as, for example, the story told by Salman to Prophet Muhammad about a man who devoted almost all his time to spiritual practices, forgetting to provide for himself and his family. When the Prophet Muhammad (ﷺ) learned that Salman had counseled the man saying, "Your Lord has a right on you, your soul has a right on you, and your family has a right on you; so you should give the rights of all those who have a right on you," the Prophet (ﷺ) then confirmed that his advice was correct (Bukhârî). Another *Hādīth* which also attests to this concern of the Prophet (ﷺ) with biological needs occurred when some of his companions, in order to increase their spirituality, told him: "I will offer the prayer throughout the night forever." The other said, "I will fast throughout the year and will not break my fast." The third said, "I will keep away from the women and will not marry forever." Allah's Messenger (ﷺ) came to them and said, "Are you the same people who said so-and-so? By Allah, I am more submissive to Allah and more afraid of Him than you; yet I fast and break my fast, I do sleep and I also marry women. So he who does not follow my tradition in religion, is not from me" (Bukhârî).

As long as it does not violate religious rules, the satisfaction of human pleasures and desires is encouraged and counted as acts of devotion. This confirms Islam's holistic nature, which, by merging spiritual life with material life, extends spirituality to all aspects of life rather than restricting it to only prayers or religious practices alone. Therefore, there are several practical possibilities within this topic that can contribute to individual well-being. According to doctrinal teachings, acts of worship (*ibadah*) are a broad field that encompasses both formal rituals and ordinary everyday acts such as eating, working, family life, sex, studies, and business, among others. This also includes pleasures and moments of entertainment, as long as they are in line with the parameters of lawfulness established by the Quran and *Sunnah*. Pleasures prohibited by Islamic law, although more desirable in human eyes than lawful pleasures, and although not considered harmful by traditional science, are avoided by Muslims both because they are prohibited and because of the belief that every divine prohibition is intended to protect human beings from something harmful to them. Muslims see illegal acts or adverse situations as true "tests of faith," since these are the occasions that will define how individuals will use their free will and spirituality.

6.2.6 Individual Well-Being at a Physical/Biological Level

Psychospiritual well-being results from harmony among the *rūḥ*, *qalb*, *aql*, and *nafs*, which will consequently also reflect on physical health. In turn, we cannot talk about psychological well-being without also including bodily health. Taking care of one's physical health is fundamental in Islam and has direct repercussions not only on the health of the body's various organs but also on psychological well-being. Physical health is, in fact, doubly related to the elements of the soul. The first relationship is between physical and spiritual health, since disobedience to such religious prescriptions and the practice of *haram* behaviors generate discomfort and a disconnection of the individual in relation to God and His *fitrah*. This contributes to the emergence of negative feelings about oneself that can, in turn, manifest or have repercussions on physical health. The second relationship is between psychological and physiological health, since a *nafs* excessively attached to matter and pleasures, incapable of developing sufficient discipline and self-control to avoid harmful behaviors, ends up affecting not only the spiritual dimension but also individuals' cognitive functions, emotional balance, and behavior, predisposing them to addictions and compulsions.

In addition to the influence of Islamic spiritual practices on health, Muslims consider the Quran itself a resource for both spiritual and physical healing, especially since, if the effects of the contents of the holy book affect the heart, they consequently have repercussions on the entire body. Although human science has not yet fully unraveled this phenomenon, Muslims often use the Quran in situations of physical illness or emotional suffering, thus combining spiritual and transcendental strength with traditional resources for treating both the physical and mental spheres.

Another important aspect regarding the body's health is Islamic recommendations related to nutrition. Islam prohibits harmful foods such as pork, blood, carrion, and the ingestion of alcohol, and recommends all that is healthy, such as seafood, meat, honey, vegetables, and fruits in general. Fasting, both mandatory and voluntary, has been encouraged in Islam, and only today has science demonstrated its benefits for both physical and psychological health. The Quran clearly recommends that humans enjoy what they are allowed, but without excess (Quran, 20:81). This emphasis on moderation is also extremely important for the body's health and equilibrium and is also one of the keys to physical and psychospiritual well-being. From a psychic point of view, excesses lead to compulsions, whether compulsions for food or those related to other pleasures such as alcohol, sex, gambling, consumption, etc. The Prophet Muhammad (ﷺ) also emphasized balance and moderation in food when he said, "A human being fills no worse vessel than his stomach. It is sufficient for a human being to eat a few mouthfuls to keep his spine straight. But if he must (fill it), then one third of food, one third for drink and one third for air" (Sunan Ibn Majah). Excessive eating can have an impact on spiritual practices due to laziness or malaise, in addition to impairing the capacity for self-control and cognitive performance (Utz, 2011).

Sexual relations restricted to marriage, reducing the spread of sexually transmitted diseases, and the prohibition of anal sex and pornography are also religious prescriptions that serve both to protect Muslims' physical and psychological health. Beautification, cleanliness, and personal hygiene are also encouraged in Islam as forms of self-care. In addition to protecting individuals from diseases and infections, they prevent them from experiencing social embarrassment due to neglect of appearance or hygiene, which also impacts self-esteem. Such guidance appears in various *Hadīths* and also in the Quran, such as in the verse that says, "Indeed, Allah loves those who are constantly recurring and loves those who purify them" (Quran, 2:222, interpretation of the meaning), and also in the *Hadīth* in which the Prophet (ﷺ) states, "Allah is Beautiful, He loves beauty." Exercising is also an important key to well-being, both physically or psychologically. The practice of some physical exercises was also recommended by the Prophet Muhammad (ﷺ). Those mentioned in the *Sunnah* include swimming, archery, horse riding, wrestling (Munsoor, 2021; Rothman, 2018), and also running, mentioned in an episode when he and his wife Aisha competed against each other.

6.2.6.1 *Qalb*: The Central Role of the Heart in Physical and Psychological Well-Being in Islam

The heart (*qalb*) is one of the structures connecting the body to the elements of the soul. It is therefore essential to know the heart's repercussions on the physical, psychological, and spiritual spheres. It is important to remember that in Islam, the heart simultaneously integrates spiritual, psychic, and physiological functions which, when combined, can affect the body's balance and health. This finding is based on both religious teachings and data from the literature already cited. According to the Hadīth of the Prophet Muhammad (ﷺ): "There is a piece of flesh in the body if it becomes good (reformed) the whole body becomes good but if it gets spoilt the whole body gets spoilt and that is the heart" (Bukhârî and Muslim). The *Hadīth* refers to the spiritual heart, but it can also be related to physical health, as cited in the psychosomatic studies of prominent philosophers such as Al-Balkhi. Somatization in distinct parts of the body, in the form of physical illnesses, has a direct relationship to emotional issues, which, from an Islamic perspective, are linked to the heart.

The heart is understood in Islam as the essence, the central spiritual and intellectual core that influences all of the body's organs. Al-Ghazali describes the heart as an immaterial structure that represents the essence of the human soul (self). According to his perspective, the heart unites an individual's body and spirit, symbolizing the physical and spiritual heart where belief, faith, and divine revelations are found. For him, this organ would be both the center of the self and that of knowledge. Hence, the emphasis on spirituality and the process of purifying the soul, which aims to keep the heart free of impurities and thus more easily receive spiritual knowledge and divine light (Munsoor, 2021).

Keshavarzi and Khan (2018) state that every type of health or illness is linked to the heart. The heart is the personality's core and what will shape it, according to an individual's conduct (Huq, 2022). This is because, in the Islamic view, it is understood that, with the exception of some functions, most behavioral responses are controlled by the heart and not by the brain. Furthermore, the prophetic quote highlights the heart as the key point for health, but it is a concept of health that goes beyond the physical dimension, also encompassing spiritual and psychological aspects. There is a holistic and integrated concept of well-being in Islam, and the presence of a unifying element that commands and reflects its condition in all others.

From an Islamic perspective, the heart is considered the point of spiritual connection between individuals and God, that is, the center of spiritual intelligence that connects humans to their pure nature, the *fitrah* (Rothman, 2022). In addition to emotions and affections, the heart is also considered an organ linked to intuition, knowledge, and perception. It is the center of cognitive and voluntary functions and is thus a "supersensory organ" (Utz, 2011, p. 73). Fear of God is only possible through purity of the heart and has a direct connection with it. Islamic doctrine understands that sins and bad deeds obscure the heart, hindering the passage of light, insights, and divine knowledge that elevate individuals to the highest level of Islamic spiritual intelligence (*ladunni*). This intelligence, granted directly by God to individuals due to their devotion and obedience, expands their intuition and perception (*firassa*), causing them to notice things that not all ordinary people would be able to (Wahab, 2022). Utz (2011) states that sinners' hearts end up distancing them from God, leaving individuals in a constant state of worry and anxiety, feelings that are opposed to psychological well-being.

The heart (*qalb*) is considered the most important structure of all for Muslims because we understand that the entire physiological and behavioral process would result from a previous process of a psychospiritual nature (Huq, 2022). If the entire body is subordinate to the heart, it is therefore responsible for human actions, since people's motivations originate from the heart. The heart (*qalb*) understands the meaning of things through the intellect (*aql*) and acts through desire (*iradah*). Thus, the intellect sediments the values and purposes that the heart will use to motivate the individual and generate desires that, in turn, will be externalized through behavior.

There is also a detail of utmost importance for the well-being of the heart: intention. Sincere intention (*niyya*) is one of the elements related to the spirit (*rūḥ*) and the heart (*qalb*). This reveals what is truly behind human actions, because even if such actions are good, the intention hidden behind them may be beneficial or harmful, as mentioned by Prophet Muhammad (ﷺ): "Deeds are to be judged only by intentions, and a man will have only what he intended" (Bukhârî and Muslim). An action performed with pure and sincere intention nourishes and illuminates the heart, unlike a false intention, which brings the individual even closer to their animal nature, weakening them and distancing them from spiritual evolution. This, in turn, impacts all other psychic structures such as human cognition, emotions, and behavior (Keshavarzi et al., 2021). The true intention of actions may not be discovered by other individuals, but God knows, as well as those who perform them, directly affecting their conscience and state of mind.

Recent discoveries about the heart–brain relationship seem to be overturning knowledge that, until now, seemed solid in traditional science. According to McCraty (2015), the heart is an organ with its own logic, which acts autonomously by issuing commands to the brain that influence individuals' perceptions, behavior, and even short- and long-term memory functions (McCraty, 2015, p. 5). There is also evidence that self-induced positive emotions, such as compassion, for example, make the heart rhythm more coherent and harmonious (McCraty & Zayas, 2014; Figueredo, 2023; Fredrickson, 2009).

Studies show that the heart's functions are so broad that they can change the function of the entire body system (McCraty et al., 2009). With more than 40,000 neurons in the heart, there is a neuronal circuit linked mainly to the vagus nerve, which connects it to the brain and other brain structures such as the thalamus, hypothalamus, and amygdala (McCraty & Zayas, 2014). The heart is not only an organ that pumps blood through the body but also has much broader and more complex functions as part of an extensive communication network with the brain and other organs in the body. The heart, like the brain, also secretes hormones and neurotransmitters linked to well-being, such as norepinephrine and dopamine (McCraty, 2015). Oxytocin, known as the hormone of love, trust, and bonding, appears to be produced in the heart in the same quantities as in the brain. There is a powerful electromagnetic field in the heart, 60 times greater than that of the brain (Figueredo, 2023), where information internal and external to the body is regulated and distributed throughout the body, influencing physiological, cognitive, emotional, and behavioral functions. Many human feelings reverberate in the heart, impacting physiological elements such as heartbeat and high blood pressure, among others. The rhythmic patterns that the heart emits reverberate throughout the body, transmitting hormonal, neurological, and electromagnetic information. There is also evidence that the heart significantly influences the brain's neurological functions and the modulation of cognitive functions such as attention, motivation, decision-making, pain perception, and emotional processing (McCraty et al., 2009; McCraty, 2015; Figueredo, 2023). These contemporary scientific findings are promising, indicating that the heart plays a far more extensive role than previously assumed, with the ability to influence and be influenced by physiological, psychological, social, environmental and also spiritual factors.

6.3 The Individual–Divine Creation Relationship (Humans and Nature)

The struggle or effort of the soul (*jihad el-nafs*) is a continuous and daily process that requires constancy, patience, attention, persistence, and firmness so that one does not succumb to the lower self's insistent desires and become spiritually lost. This internal struggle, however, not only involves a life of isolation but is above all linked to individuals' relationships with their peers. If we consider that much of human suffering results from individuals' behavior or from those with whom they live in their environment, we can then see the importance of understanding the process of character development, the practice of virtues, and the purification of the soul for individuals' and society's emotional health (Omais et al., 2023). Social life becomes rather difficult if there is no code of conduct that reinforces ethics and morals. The moral psychology that exists in the Muslim holy book is one of the great pillars for the construction of just and sensitive individuals (Bakhtiar, 2019). It is no wonder that the Quran lists a series of virtues that are important for social relationships, such as justice, civic spirit, generosity, responsibility, compassion, kindness, love, cooperation, confidentiality, humanity, and various prosocial behaviors (Bensaid et al., 2014; Omais et al., 2023). Practicing these virtues can be an important resource to achieve spiritual and psychological well-being.

The practice of virtues and good deeds in Islam is more aligned with a social than an individualistic vision (Tajul Ariffin et al., 2022). This is why Muslims sometimes sacrifice individual pleasure or wealth in the name of higher social or spiritual values, since individual happiness would not be possible without collective happiness (Joshanloo, 2017). From an Islamic perspective, individual well-being reflects social well-being, and vice versa. For Rassool (2021), social cognition is a psychological process focused on understanding both individuals and their peers. According to him, there is a certain consensus in the literature about the relationship between social and religious cognition, given that the latter has contents that reflect on the social environment.

By focusing on the common good and not just on individual satisfaction, we have a result that, over time, can have a positive impact on everyone. However, practicing virtues consistently is a difficult habit to maintain in the long term, requiring a skill that is highly encouraged in Islam: self-discipline. Self-discipline is present in various spiritual practices such as praying at the proper times, fasting, eating halal, and hygiene practices, among others (Rothman, 2018). Thus, it is not enough to simply understand the importance of good behavior, but rather to practice it until virtue is integrated into individuals' way of being (Rahim, 2013). To do this, a reason is needed to sustain this practice, since it often requires effort, abdication, or, at certain times, a sacrifice of one's own desires for the sake of others, aiming at divine satisfaction. Therefore, in Islam, the practice of good deeds must first and foremost be anchored in belief, faith, spiritual knowledge, fear, love, and submission to God. Understanding these elements is the main motivator for behavioral change, to overcome vices, and to facilitate emotional management.

Many Muslim philosophers considered the science of ethics and morals to be the basis of all human sciences. When both are connected to faith, they make collective well-being a greater priority than individual well-being. Therefore, Bensaid et al. (2014) emphasize that the practice of virtues and good deeds must go beyond the individual dimension, but this requires habit, constancy, and practice. Training is necessary to modify and improve certain behaviors. Al-Ghazali believed in the possibility of changing human beings through training, just as when animal behavior is modified through training (Munsoor, 2021). However, training the soul needs to be carried out alongside improvement of character and good conduct, as we can see in Fig. 6.7.

Improving human behavior is one of the paths to both individual and collective well-being, since it positively affects interactions among people, and this has repercussions for individuals, and vice versa. There is an inverse relationship between spirituality and individualism in certain cultures, and one explanation for this may be the fact that socialization is also a form of spirituality, of connecting with God (Keshavarzi & Khan, 2018). This is another point that differentiates Islamic psychology from Western positive psychology, since in Islam, the practice of virtues and prosocial behaviors is not only aimed at individuals' well-being but, above all, at the social context, benefiting and positively impacting the entire community and the environment.

Most psychological approaches still focus on the material dimension, sensations, desires, autonomy, and unlimited free will, rather than focusing on what differentiates human beings from animals: rationality and spirituality. Now, if hedonism, in addition to not generating lasting happiness and being the root of many dysfunctional and compulsive behaviors that use pleasure as an "escape valve" for life's problems, it is at the very least incongruent and contradictory that psychology, a

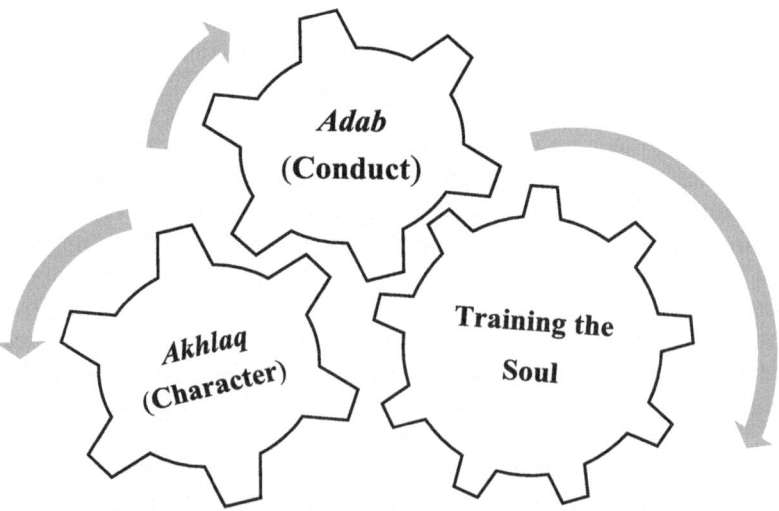

Fig. 6.7 The training of the soul *(Riyadat el-nafs)*

science aiming at individuals' mental and emotional health, uses theories based on the principle of "pleasure" and the satisfaction of individuals' desires, making them slaves to their passions and desires instead of teaching them to tame their impulses. The focus on the satisfaction of human desires stimulates the immediate and hedonic culture in which we live. This reduces individuals' ability to adjust to certain limits, to respect boundaries and social rules, to postpone gratification, and to assume a less individualistic and self-centered position. How can we develop prosocial skills in a society where individuals are taught and encouraged to think only about satisfying their needs? How can we expand the social paradigm in psychology if the language of theoretical approaches is focused on attributes that, for the most part, are still linked to the word "self," such as self-esteem, self-love, self-confidence, self-efficacy, self-fulfillment, self-sufficiency, self-realization, self-satisfaction, self-worth, self-respect, and self-compassion?

Western psychological language shows how strongly it is still connected to individualism. With the exception of words like "empathy" or "compassion," which do not always carry the same weight as other more individual terms, you can see how much Western psychological vocabulary has developed around the idea of the self. Vocabulary is very much a reflection of a society's values, and a closer look at the language we use in psychology shows explicitly how Western society is still immersed in individualism. This is a reality that has progressively increased with secularization. So, if we need to rethink even the language in science—given that vocabulary is so extensively developed around the idea of the self, but very little in social terminology—how can we convey the idea that collective well-being is as important as individual well-being? Although psychology is a science that studies individuals' psyche, this does not justify it having such an individual outlook, so centered on the self, not least because if this is a science that is part of both human and social sciences, then the social factor should be one of its main bases.

In addition to the social context and the importance of harmony in human relationships for well-being, we should emphasize that virtuous behavior and good deeds are not restricted to the human species alone, but are practices that can and should be directed toward any and all living beings, such as animals, plants, and the whole environment where we live. In Islam, individuals' commitment to other living beings is not only linked to their lives but also to their Creator. Therefore, humans assume a double responsibility in their external relations: one toward the beings and the other toward the One who created them.

The fact that all beings' well-being, whether human or not, is a duty not only to them but above all to God creates a sense of commitment formed both by empathy toward the other and by fear of harming a being who is in divine custody and to Whom human beings will also be accountable if their behavior is inappropriate or unjust. Several Ḥadīths emphasize the importance of this when the Prophet Muhammad (ﷺ) said, "There is a reward for serving any animate (living being)" (Bukhârî). In another Ḥadīth, the Prophet (ﷺ) said, "Be merciful on the earth, and you will be shown mercy from Who is above the heavens" (Tirmidhî). He also reinforced the impact that treating living beings well has on individuals when he said that "Whoever is kind to the creatures of God is kind to himself" (Bukhârî).

Individuals' relationships with other beings encompass nature, animals, and also human beings. The aim here is to equalize the importance of any living being, reinforcing the need to behave appropriately toward all of them, whether human or nonhuman. In Islam, *adab* is owed equally to all beings, and we will be held accountable for our actions. Furthermore, since good conduct and behavior have a direct impact on well-being, it is important that this relationship be healthy, harmonious, and respectful.

Prophet Muhammad (ﷺ) emphasized that the relationship between human beings and other creatures—whether human or not—is an important part of belief. There is a Ḥadīth in which he states, "You will not have secure faith until you love one another and have mercy on those who live upon the earth" (Bukhârî). The Ḥadīths use generic terms such as "creatures of God" or "those who live upon the Earth." Therefore, following the wisdom of the *Sunnah*, I have also used in the *Islamic Triadic Model of Well-Being* the term in this more generic sense to encompass individuals' external relationships with other creatures, thus conferring the same status of importance on both human beings and other beings in nature, even though there are obviously different types of relationships within this group. We should emphasize that humanity is at a point where concern for human well-being depends entirely on a balanced environment, and there is a pressing need for this issue to be given the same importance as the care that we must take in human relations. The aim is not to superimpose the environment on human relationships, but to build a model of well-being that includes all types of relationships human beings establish externally with the world as equally relevant. The expression "Divine Creation" or "God's Creation," in addition to encompassing all living beings without distinction, equalizing all creatures, ends up highlighting the importance of all of them and encouraging virtuous conduct such as love, generosity, and compassion, which have a positive impact on individuals and social well-being, and also on the environment.

6.4 The Pyramidal Model of Well-Being: A Model That Combines the Islamic Triadic Model of Well-Being and the Quranic Model for a Pleasant Life

After thoroughly understanding the concepts and models presented throughout this and the previous chapters, it is possible to propose a model that consolidates the key elements related to well-being in Islam. The Pyramidal Model of Well-Being in Islam, presented in Fig. 6.8, synthesizes the spiritual factors that shape an individual's relationships from a holistic perspective of well-being, combining both internal and external dimensions.

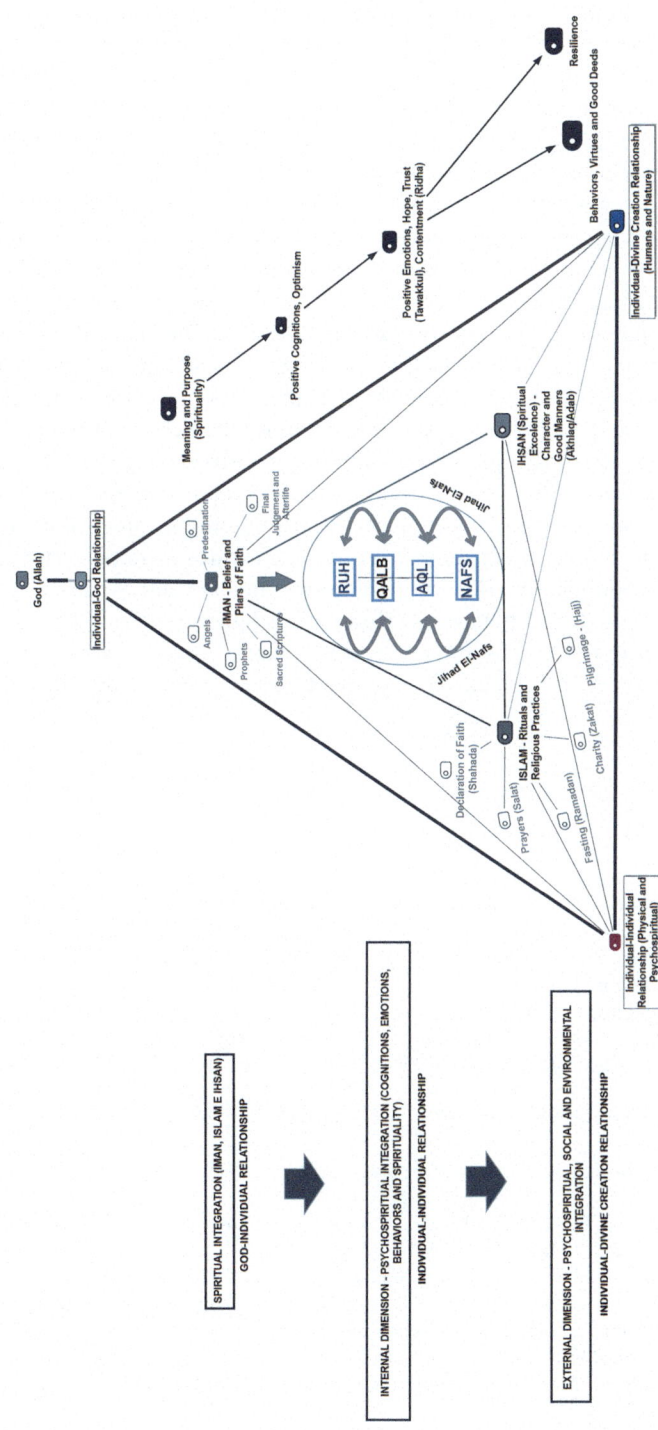

Fig. 6.8 The Pyramidal Model of Well-Being in Islam and the spiritual elements that influence the individual's relationships—Elaborated by the author

The pyramidal model summarizes all the items previously discussed throughout this and earlier chapters, bringing together the fundamental elements that connect Islamic spirituality with well-being. The integration and connection established between faith (*Iman*), practices and rituals (*Islam*), and spiritual excellence (*Ihsan*), alongside an individual's relationships with God, with themselves, and with all of God's creation, form the fundamental foundation for a dynamic balance between the elements of the soul. In other words, the foundation of belief is built on faith (*Iman*) and its pillars, which give purpose and meaning to both the spiritual and worldly actions of a Muslim. This belief, alongside Islamic practices, rituals, and the pursuit of spiritual excellence (*Ihsan*), encourages the Muslim to refine their character and behavior in relation to others and to God. Together, these elements form the basis of psycho-spiritual balance and harmony within the soul's internal aspects: *ruh, qalb, aql, and nafs*. Achieving this integration requires personal effort and spiritual growth (*jihad al-nafs*), striving to control the desires of the *nafs* and to improve one's character (*akhlaq*) through alignment with divine guidance and virtuous behavior. At this stage, the individual can foster more positive relationships, supported by the integration of their internal spiritual dimension with the external dimensions of environment and society. This cycle creates a framework that links spiritual and psychological well-being to a more collective and expansive perspective, encompassing external behaviors. However, achieving internal balance is the initial step for an individual to attain external balance, as the absence of a stable emotional and spiritual foundation can make social interactions difficult and challenging.

References

Al Jawziyya, I. Q. (2020). *Ranks of divine seekers* (O. Anjum Trad.). Brill.

Al-Attas, S. M. N. (1995). *Prolegomena to the metaphysics of Islam: An exposition of the fundamental elements of the worldview of Islam*. International Institute of Islamic Thought and Civilization (ISTAC).

Alias, A., & Samsudin, M. Z. (2005). Psychology of motivation from an Islamic perspective. *3rd International Seminar onLearning and Motivation, 10*, 12. https://www.researchgate.net/publication/338593508_PSYCHOLOGY_OF_MOTIVATION_FROM_AN_ISLAMIC_PERSPECTIVE

Al-Qarni, A. A. (2005). *Don't be sad* (F. I. M. Shafeeq Trad., 2nd ed.). International Islamic Publishing House.

Bakhtiar, L. (2019). *Quranic psychology of the self: A text book on Islamic moral psychology*. Kazi Publications.

Bensaid, B., Machouche, S., & Grine, F. (2014). A Qur'anic framework for spiritual intelligence. *Religions, 5*(1), 179–198. https://doi.org/10.3390/rel5010179

Bukhârî and Muslim. Mishkat al-Masabih 1. Sunnah.com. https://sunnah.com/mishkat:1

Bukhârî and Muslim. Riyad as-Salihin 587. Sunnah.com. https://sunnah.com/riyadussalihin:587

Bukhârî. Sahih al-Bukhari 2466. In-book reference: Book 46, Hādīth 27. Sunnah.com. https://sunnah.com/bukhari:2466

Bukhârî. Sahih al-Bukhari 5063. In-book reference: Book 67, Hādīth 1. Sunnah.com. https://sunnah.com/bukhari:5063

Bukhârî. Sahih al-Bukhari 6139. In-book reference: Book 78, Ḥadīth 166. Sunnah.com. https:// sunnah.com/bukhari:6139

Cohn, M. A., Fredrickson, B. L., Brown, S. L., Mikels, J. A., & Conway, A. M. (2009). Happiness unpacked: Positive emotions increase life satisfaction by building resilience. *Emotion, 9*(3), 361–368. https://doi.org/10.1037/a0015952

Figueredo, V. M. (2023). *The curious history of the heart: A cultural and scientific journey.* Columbia University Press.

Fredrickson, B. L. (2001). The role of positive emotions in positive psychology: The broaden-and-build theory of positive emotions. *American Psychologist, 56*(3), 218–226. https://doi.org/1 0.1037//0003-066x.56.3.218

Fredrickson, B. L. (2009). *Positividade: Descubra A Força das Emoções Positivas, Supere a Negatividade e Viva Plenamente.* Rocco.

Fredrickson, B. L. (2013). Positive emotions broaden and build. In P. Devine & A. Plant (Eds.), *Advances in experimental social psychology* (Vol. 47, pp. 1–53). Academic Press. https://doi. org/10.1016/B978-0-12-407236-7.00001-2

Huq, M. (2022). The heart and personality development. In A. Haque & Y. Mohamed (Eds.), *Psychology of personality: Islamic perspectives* (pp. 135–153). International Association of Islamic Psychology.

Joshanloo, M. (2017). Islamic conceptions of well-being. In R. Estes & M. Sirgy (Eds.), *The pursuit of human well-being. International handbooks of quality-of-life.* Springer. https://doi. org/10.1007/978-3-319-39101-4_5

Joshanloo, M., & Weijers, D. (2019). Islamic perspectives on well-being. In L. Lambert & N. Pasha-Zaidi (Eds.), *Positive psychology in the Middle East/North Africa.* Springer. https:// doi.org/10.1007/978-3-030-13921-6_11

Keshavarzi, H., & Khan, F. (2018). Outlining a case illustration of traditional islamically integrated psychotherapy (TIIP). In C. Y. Al-Karam (Ed.), *Islamically integrated psychotherapy: Uniting faith and professional practice* (pp. 175–207). Templeton Press.

Keshavarzi, H., & Nsour, R. (2021). Behavioral (*Nafsānī*) psychotherapy: Character development and reformation. In H. Keshavarzi, F. Khan, B. Ali, & R. Awaad (Eds.), *Applying Islamic principles to clinical mental health care. Introducing Traditional Islamically Integrated Psychotherapy* (pp. 236–265). Routledge.

Keshavarzi, H., Khan, F., Ali, B., & Awaad, R. (2021). *Applying Islamic principles to clinical mental health care. Introducing Traditional Islamically Integrated Psychotherapy.* Routledge.

Khalil, A. (2014). Contentment, satisfaction and good-pleasure: Rida in early Sufi moral psychology. *Studies in Religion/Sciences Religieuses, 43*(3), 371–389. https://doi. org/10.1177/0008429814538227

McCraty, R. (2015). *Science of the heart: Exploring the role of the heart in human performance* (Vol. 2). HeartMath Institute.

McCraty, R., & Zayas, M. A. (2014). Cardiac coherence, self-regulation, autonomic stability, and psychosocial well-being. *Frontiers in Psychology, 5*, 1090. https://doi.org/10.3389/ fpsyg.2014.01090

McCraty, R., Atkinson, M., Tomasino, D., & Bradley, R. T. (2009). *The coherent heart: Heart-brain interactions, psychophysiological coherence, and the emergence of system-wide order.* HeartMath Institute.

Munsoor, M. S. (2021). *Wellbeing and the worshipper.* Springer.

Muslim. Riyad as-Salihin 27. In-book reference: Introduction, Ḥadīth 27. Sunnah.com. https:// sunnah.com/riyadussalihin:27

Muslim. Riyad as-Salihin 611. Sunnah.com. https://sunnah.com/riyadussalihin:611

Omais, S., Tarif, E., & Santos, M. A. (2023). Ethics, morals, virtues and character strengths: A comparison between Islamic psychology and positive psychology. In C. Y. Al-Karam (Ed.), *The way of love* (pp. 129–152). Al Karam Press.

Rahim, A. B. A. (2013). Understanding Islamic ethics and its significance on the character building. *International Journal of Social Science and Humanity, 3*(6), 508–513. https://doi.org/10.7763/IJSSH.2013.V3.293

Rashid, T., & Seligman, M. (2019). *Psicoterapia Positiva: Manual do Terapeuta.* Artmed.

Rassool, G. H. (2021). *Islamic psychology: Human behaviour and experience from an Islamic perspective.* Routledge.

Rothman, A. (2018). An Islamic theoretical orientation to psychotherapy. In C. Y. Al-Karam (Ed.), *Islamically integrated psychotherapy: Uniting faith and professional practice* (pp. 25–56). Templeton Press.

Rothman, A. (2022). *Developing a model of Islamic psychology and psychotherapy: Islamic theology and contemporary understandings of psychology.* Routledge.

Rothman, A., & Coyle, A. (2018). Toward a framework for Islamic psychology and psychotherapy: An Islamic model of the soul. *Journal of Religion and Health, 57*(5), 1731–1744. https://doi.org/10.1007/s10943-018-0651-x

Sholichatun, Y. (2023). The comparison of acceptance and Ridha. *Proceedings of the Second Conference on Psychology and Flourishing Humanity, Advances in Social Science, Education and Humanities Research, 808.* https://doi.org/10.2991/978-2-38476-188-3_2

Sunan Ibn Majah. In-book reference: Book 29, Hādīth 99. Sunnah.com. https://sunnah.com/ibnmajah:3349

Tajul Ariffin, A. H., AbdulKhaiyom, J. H., & Rosli, A. N. (2022). Islam, Iman, and Ihsan: The role of religiosity on quality of life and mental health of Muslim undergraduate students. *IIUM Medical Journal Malaysia, 21*(3), 146–154. https://doi.org/10.31436/imjm.v21i3.2047

The Clear Quran. (n.d.). (M. Khattab, Trans.). https://quran.com/

Tirmidhî. Jami' at-Tirmidhi 1924. In-book reference: Book 27, Hādīth 30. Sunnah.com. https://sunnah.com/tirmidhi:1924

Tirmidhî. Jami' at-Tirmidhi 2151. In-book reference: Book 32, Hādīth 19. Sunnah.com. https://sunnah.com/tirmidhi:2151

Tirmidhî. Jami' at-Tirmidhi 2305. In-book reference: Book 36, Hādīth 2. Sunnah.com. https://sunnah.com/tirmidhi:2305

Utz, A. (2011). *Psychology from Islamic perspective.* International Islamic Publishing House.

Van Cappellen, P., Edwards, M. E., Kamble, S. V., Yildiz, M., & Ladd, K. L. (2024). Kneel, stand, prostrate: The psychology of prayer postures in three world religions. *PLoS One, 19*(8), e0306924. https://doi.org/10.1371/journal.pone.0306924

Van Cappellen, P., Zhang, R., & Fredrickson, B. L. (2023). The scientific study of positive emotions and religion/spirituality. In E. B. Davis, E. L. Worthington Jr., & S. A. Schnitker (Eds.), *Handbook of positive psychology, religion, and spirituality* (pp. 315–328). Springer.

Vishkin, A., Ben-Nun Bloom, P., Schwartz, S. H., Solak, N., & Tamir, M. (2019). Religiosity and emotion regulation. *Journal of Cross-Cultural Psychology, 50*(9), 1050–1074. https://doi.org/10.1177/0022022119880341

Wahab, M. A. (2022). Islamic spiritual and emotional intelligence and its relationship to eternal happiness: A conceptual paper. *Journal of Religion and Health, 61*(6), 4783–4806. https://doi.org/10.1007/s10943-021-01485-2

Wiliasih, R., Siregar, H., Irawan, T., & Beik, I. S. (2024). Happiness in Islam and influencing factors (SLR approach). *Al-Muzara'ah – Journal of Islamic Economics & Finance, 12*(1), 137–157. https://doi.org/10.29244/jam.12.1.137-157

Chapter 7
Final Considerations

The study of happiness and well-being is connected to different fields of psychological science. Classical psychological theories disseminated in the West often considered religion to be a dispensable object in individuals' lives and a hindrance to their evolution, showing a certain resistance to, or even embarrassment in, using the term "religion" as a positive element for mental health. For a long time, psychology reduced the importance of religion and spirituality in the study of the human psyche, giving them a more negative and pathological representation. Psychological science has even created this separation in its nomenclature, exchanging the term "soul" for the term psyche or self, as if the two were different and separable structures. Reducing religion only to an institutional or doctrinal dimension can create a partial knowledge that, in the end, disregards the many benefits it can generate in individuals' lives.

While Western science fragments knowledge into different areas of psychology, the conception of well-being in Islamic psychology integrates content from various approaches simultaneously, connecting beliefs, religious teachings, spiritual practices, morals, ethics, and prosocial behaviors, based on a logic in which God, the individual, and society are closely related to each other. Some of the ideas discussed in this book may conflict with Western theories and paradigms, which are still almost exclusively focused on an individual-centered view that prioritizes individual desires and impulses over values, beliefs, spirituality, and religious rules. Ignoring the religious precepts that patients believe in and "secularizing" their behaviors as if these beliefs were dysfunctional or obsolete can generate a superficial therapeutic approach that is distant from individuals' real world. A cognitive reframing conducted by a therapist who simply prioritizes the satisfaction of individual needs without a holistic view, superimposing them on values and spiritual orientations that are significant to the client, is an invasive and incoherent approach. This is where secular psychological currents diverge in relation to psychospiritual epistemologies, and the same applies to the study of well-being. Although this scenario is changing, based on modern theories that include environmental and sociocultural influences, the individual paradigm still prevails.

Although well-being in Islam can be represented in different ways, in general, there are many points in common among the various proposals in the Islamic literature, especially with regard to the internal dynamics of the soul's elements and the search for balance among reason, the heart, the spirit, the mind, the behavior, and

S. Omais, *Happiness and Well-Being in Islam*,
https://doi.org/10.1007/978-3-031-95353-8_7

the body. That balance, when externalized in the form of conduct and actions, in turn, has repercussions on both society and the individual themselves.

However, despite the integration of all these facets (and others that fall within each of them), this work has shown that it is also possible to summarize Islamic well-being in two essential themes: belief/faith and good deeds. Throughout this book, special emphasis has been placed on the Quranic verse that mentions the ingredients of a pleasant life (Quran 16:97). The word "believer" refers to the individual's important relationship with God, the basis of which are the pillars of faith, on which is anchored the entire foundation of cognitions and meanings that will engage and motivate him to action. Strengthening faith and the spiritual dimension are the starting point for change in Islam. Any external behavior first requires an internal change, as the Quranic verse teaches when it reminds us that "Indeed, Allāh will not change the condition of a people until they change what is in themselves" (13:11). Faith represents *Iman*, while good deeds represent both *Islam*, which encompasses the rituals and religious practices themselves, and *Ishan*, which encourages excellence and individuals' spiritual evolution. Good deeds are the externalization and concretization of faith in practical and real terms, generating benefits for both the individual and society, harmonizing and strengthening their relationships with other beings and also with God.

The Qur'anic Model for a Pleasant Life simplifies the concept of well-being, allowing professionals to explore with clients individuals' strengths within these two dimensions. It aligns spiritual beliefs with the practice of virtues in order to enhance and unite the development of human qualities with individuals' spiritual evolution. On the other hand, the Islamic *Triadic Model of Well-Being* is based on three closely interconnected relationships that are essential for mental health.

Because it is a relational model, the pillars of the Islamic *Triadic Model of Well-Being* are the relationships humans establish in the spiritual sphere, connecting with aspects related to the psychic, social, and environmental dimensions, as opposed to traditional perspectives on well-being that focus almost exclusively on individuals and their needs. The model's focus is to enable a vision of well-being that results from the healthy relationship among individuals, God, and other creatures, whether human or not. It is a proposal that includes the spiritual, individual (psychological and physical), social, and environmental dimensions together.

A healthy connection between individuals and God comes about by strengthening faith and belief. This is consolidated through knowledge, faith (*Iman*), obedience, and full trust in God (*tawakkul*), reading and reciting the Quran, remembrance of God (*dhikr*), prayer, repentance (*tawbah*), and other spiritual practices. Strengthening the spiritual dimension, in turn, has a positive impact on the other two dimensions: the individual–individual relationship and the individual–Divine Creation relationship.

The individual–individual relationship focuses on intrapsychic health, which can be strengthened through connection with God and spiritual practices, as well as by contemplative practices (*taffakur*), self-reflection, self-care, contentment (*ridha*), spiritual effort (*jihad el-nafs*), lawful behavior (*halal*) and the avoidance of unlawful behavior (*haram*), the strengthening of character, and physical health care.

The individual–Divine Creation relationship is strengthened through individuals' relationships with other beings, both human and nonhuman. Virtuous, moral, and ethical behavior (*akhlaq* and *adab*), and good deeds encompass a multitude of possible interventions that can be used as practices to positively nurture these relationships from a family, emotional, and social point of view, as well as individuals' relationships with animals, plants, nature, and the environment in general. Islam emphasizes respect for all creatures on Earth. Therefore, harmonious and respectful relationships between individuals and the world around them are fundamental to well-being.

The *Pyramidal Model of Well-Being in Islam*, proposed in this book, integrates the spiritual, psychological, physical, social, and environmental aspects. The model synthesizes the spiritual factors that shape the individual's relationships from a holistic perspective of well-being that combines internal and external dimensions. In order to attain balance across all these dimensions, the individual must actively work on their spiritual growth and refine their behavior and character.

Understanding this worldview can help professionals identify the points of strength and weakness that affect clients' mental health, thus enabling a more comprehensive psychological treatment focused on these relationships' harmonious balance and on Islam's holistic perspective. The limitations regarding the proposals presented in this book relate mainly to the experimental aspect, which is why future research is needed to verify the effectiveness of therapeutic interventions based on this model. However, the ideas that served as the foundation for the construction of these models stem from studies by various authors in the field, including the research of the author herself, whose findings converge at several points. The models and discussions presented throughout this book point the way for the creation of tests and instruments to measure well-being, as well as psychological interventions and clinical practices focused specifically on Muslims' beliefs.

With regard to emotions, we have observed throughout this book that satisfaction and tranquility seem to be the most valued emotional states associated with happiness in worldly life and can be achieved through strong faith and good deeds in line with religious norms. Islamic resources and teachings related directly or indirectly to the emotional aspect converge toward low-intensity emotions, that is, feelings of satisfaction, peace, calm, serenity, and tranquility. It is thus clear that Islam's focus is on emotional balance and neutrality, and not on oscillations or excesses, whether of positive or negative emotions.

Peace and tranquility are emotions that oppose the restlessness generated by stress, which today is one of the greatest sources of physical illness in the world. Peace and tranquility are emotions that also oppose the worry generated by anguish and anxiety. They oppose the despair generated by fear and insecurity. They oppose the affliction generated by doubt and uncertainty, as well as the deep feeling of sadness and hopelessness generated by depression. Peace, satisfaction, and tranquility are Islamic concepts of happiness that oppose the insatiable search for hedonic pleasures, generated by the need for ever higher levels of dopamine to achieve brief and superficial positive emotional peaks that, instead of providing a continuous and prolonged state of well-being, generate instability and contribute to the emergence of various compulsions, whether for food, drugs, alcohol, shopping, sex, or gambling, among others.

It is important to remember that peace is the root of the word that names the Islamic religion, which is also the root of the word that gives Muslims their name, and of the greeting that all followers of Islam, from the most diverse cultures and in the most diverse contexts, say to each other on a daily basis. Peace is the characteristic of Islam from beginning to end and is present in all its dimensions. A conscience (*aql*) and spirit (*rūḥ*) at peace result in a heart (*qalb*) at peace. A heart at peace generates balance and emotional neutrality, helping solve problems and enabling the making of better decisions. A heart at peace has an impact on physical health, homeostasis, and the stability of physiological functions. A heart at peace has an impact on social behavior, on relationships between human beings and their peers, and also with nature, animals, and divine creation. A heart at peace generates well-being in its broadest form, encompassing the mind, soul, body, and society as a whole. Peace is the cure for many ills, be they spiritual, psychological, physical, or social. Peace is the element that is most present in Islam, from the etymology of its name to its deepest doctrinal teachings. And perhaps it is on peace that science and human beings need to focus their efforts so that all people can truly achieve happiness and well-being.

Index

The manufacturer's authorised representative in the EU is Springer
Nature Customer Service Centre GmbH, Europaplatz 3, 69115 Heidelberg,
Germany. If you have any concerns regarding our products, please
contact ProductSafety@springernature.com

Printed and bound by CPI Group (UK) Ltd, Croydon, CR0 4YY

28/08/2025

01945963-0002